THE CHRISTIAN SOLDIER

The Believer's Battle

WAYNE ST. AUBYN
TULLOCH

Copyright © 2026 by Wayne St. Aubyn Tulloch. All rights reserved. Printed in the United States of America. No part of this book may be used or reproduced in any manner whatsoever without written permission except in the case of reprints in the contexts of reviews.

ISBN: 979-8-218-23658-8

Library of Congress Control Number: 2023912563

Attention: Churches, schools, and businesses:
Books are available at quantity discounts with bulk purchases for educational, business, or sales promotional use. For information, please email wtullo1@gmail.com or visit waynetulloch.com to place orders.

THE CHRISTIAN SOLDIER

WAYNE ST. AUBYN
TULLOCH

To my fellow
    brethren in the
        body of Christ.

Thou therefore endure hardness, as a good soldier of Jesus Christ. No man that warreth entangleth himself with the affairs of this life; that he may please him who hath chosen him to be a soldier.

2 Timothy 2:3-4

Preface

In the face of a diminishing world where evil appears to be conquering good, the war of circumstances direct decisions, and the deceptive fog of life blurs the vision, The Christian Soldier—born out of a passion for souls—acknowledges and illustrates the battle of the spiritual in the physical by comparing the armies of the world with the Kingdom of God. In that regard, aspects of the protagonist's endeavors are demonstrated followed by a commentary on the probable reasons for the sordid reciprocation that equates to her actions. It is hoped that the content of this book will nudge the backslider, reconverting him or her to the former state in the Kingdom, bring awareness to the unbeliever of his or her spiritual state, and strengthen the believer in the spiritual pathway.

Table of Contents

The War of Good and Evil 9

Evil Forces in Land, Sea, and Air 25

Spiritual and Physical Fundamentals 37

Physical and Spiritual Connection 53

The Armor 63

Order of Battle 81

The Battle Cry and Assault 99

Impact 115

Pressing Towards the Mark 121

A Higher Place of Praise 131

The Anointed Believer 137

Other books

"Philosophies of The Heart" 159

"Strong Men Cry, Too".. .. .. .167

"Stone Speech" 177

Chapter One
The War of Good and Evil

It was a cold winter afternoon. The dark overcast sky sent signals of another snowstorm. The shuddering crowd of commuters, draped in heavy, dark coats that matched the backdrop of the sky, stood on the station's platform in desperate anticipation as the train slowed in on the distant track. Here, amidst the gloomy crowd, I stood, with mittened hands crossed and tucked under my armpits. The clean, fresh scent of perfume, other than mine, hugged the atmosphere as the crisp, unwelcomed wind blew. My cheeks crimsoned and felt numb. I shivered and hugged myself tighter at the slightest breath of air.

As though I had all-seeing eyes, I caught the innocent eyes of a toddler in a stroller, staring at me as she tugged the hem of a commuter's coat. The mother, seemingly unconcerned, had her eyes fastened on the approaching train. It surprised me that the mother did not have a weather-shield over the stroller at this time of the year. Nevertheless, deciding that it was none of my business, I looked at the child with swift disinterest as my eyes roamed the shuddering crowd.

However, it was as though I could feel the child's penetrating stare burning through the side of my head, and, as much as I was accustomed to stares, I couldn't help turning my head to glance at her. I comforted myself with the thought that the child was not crying, which suggests she might have been comfortable, and so, my eyes kept wandering. I consoled myself further with the thought that people stared at me all the time. I was once told that I looked like the African American version of Pocahontas—a compliment that gave birth to a tinge of haughtiness. I chuckled at the thought that the child might have seen the movie on television and have mistaken me for the Native, or better yet, the Disney character.

My thoughts drifted from the child and the dull attired crowd into unchartered anatomical crevices, wandered through the trenches, and carried me to places where sensually impure imaginations erupted and held me captive.

I was on my way home to my rented apartment in Harlem, went on the wrong side of the track, took the wrong train, and ended up in Jamaica, Queens. When I realized that I was going the wrong direction, instead of correcting the error, I just kept going. Seizing the opportunity to free my mind, and to break free from the monotonous drag and the stresses of study.

So here I am, at the rails in Jamaica, waiting on the train to return to the city.

The cold months at Teachers College Columbia University proved to be a bit of a bore and so I sought someplace interesting to be, or someone interesting to talk to, someone with whom I could share my private thoughts, listen to, and flirt, even for a moment. It was my first time in New York City for an extended period and so, I wanted to explore, restaurant hop, roam Broadway, visit a bar or two, or even the museums. I felt like drifting from the academic environment and dissolving into the melting pot of a culture I had heard so much about. I yearned for a mixture—an intoxicated blend of the surreal and reality. I wanted a full dose of what the melting pot had to offer, but I needed company, someone to share with.

Then he appeared.

Drunk.

Wearing a short bright red open front jacket, with white shirt and trousers that contrasted sharply with the grey sky and dull-attired commuters on the train platform.

Who wears white in winter? I thought and noticed him further. His unkempt hair stuck from under the white hat like that of a scarecrow on a pole during harvest time. Having nothing better that I wished to do, I looked at him with growing interest a while longer. His trousers sagged below the butt. *A typical hoodlum,* I thought, as I looked him up and down.

Wearing pearly white sneakers with bright red streaks, he stood about five feet eleven inches tall—dark, and ugly.

I judged him superficially with poor discernment. This was the kind my mother warned me about. 'The scum of society,' as mom would have said.

My mother was a proper woman, a psychologist by profession, yet I left Boston, Massachusetts, and came to New York to escape her; therefore, I quickly dismissed the thoughts of her and peered at the subject in question with renewed interest.

The Ugly Drunk shook hands with an elderly Caucasian man who was smartly attired in suit and tie, unequivocally his opposite. And, they began to speak eloquently of the Stock Market, and on trading, and investments. It seemed as though the men knew each other, given the ease and relaxation with which they communicated with each other.

As I watched, the neatly attired fellow took out his notepad from his breast pocket, asked the Drunk a few questions, then scribble on the pad.

The scum of a drunk began to pique my interest. His use of rhetorical speech was attention grabbing and motivating. His repetitious punchlines were captivating. His earnest appeal-of-a-call to invest was inspiring and thought provoking—and, his perky attitude and mannerism were infectious and inviting. Commuters squeezed in to eavesdrop. I was not superior to the eavesdroppers, I decided that he was the opposite of what he looked like and what I had judged him to be; therefore, my curiosity sublimed.

I mulled over the men's exchange, captivated by their discourse which was interspersed with familiar business terminologies. I was reminded of my mother's house where several similar exchanges between my visiting uncles and her had taken place. The unearth memories acted like magnets and so I inched closer to listen.

The tantalizing fumes of alcohol on the Drunk's breath and the smell of smoke on his garments permeated his space. I thought it impossibly improbable, that this soliloquy speaking stud, standing straight, high-chested, much more majestic than most, could spearhead such conscious conversation with the wit and grace with which he did—it was mind boggling. It was mind boggling that out of the seemingly impaired mind came sound reasonings and logics.

Again, my intuition pushed me to reflect on one of my mother's proverbial statements, *'Jasmine, a bitter spring cannot bring sweet water.'* The train pulled up and we went aboard. The conversations continued, and a few others joined in. They laughed, listened, learned, and questioned the Drunk as if he were a funny professor who mixed humor with enlightenment in his classroom.

I was engulfed in the strange occurrence until I was brought to consciousness with a tug on my hand—the mother with the child in the stroller was standing next to me; the child had wrapped its tiny hand around my pinky, tugging and looking up at me with what I might have described as the cutest smile. I smiled back. Her smile changed into a chuckle, as she wagged her head from side to side as if she was telling me, *no*.

The train reached Penn Station terminal. Many of the passengers gave the Ugly Drunk nods of approval as they departed into different directions. *This was an intriguing book that could not be judged by the cover. Nothing is what it seemed. Truth is really relative,* I thought, as I mulled over the mystified encounter. I believed that I could now prove my mother wrong; my experience with this Drunk in the big city bore holes into her theory—that what you wear, is who you are, and that what you see on the outside is a striking resemblance of what lies within.

The next day, at the same time, I traveled deliberately, with expectancy, to Jamaica, Queens. And, at the rail, I intentionally peered through the precipitation, through the darkness that had descended. I peered through the mist, shivering in the cold. I looked hopefully for red and white, amongst shades of gray.

The preceding anecdote is one of many occurrences with a theme of subtle deception that an ordinary observer would probably fail to recognize at first glance. In contrast to Jasmine's mother's proverbial speech, there is an adage that says, 'looks are deceiving,' which is the same as saying, one should not judge a person or thing by the outward appearances. Here, the impetus for judging by the outward appearance was neutralized when the paradox was presented in human form. In that, the outward adornment of the Ugly Drunk already suggested that he was a typical hoodlum and a so-called scum of society, but to the commuters' amazement, his eloquence provided him the capital that bought him their listening ears. And, if that was not enough, the smartly attired elderly gentleman's endorsement and humility in taking notes and financial advice from him, gave him the credence needed to be seen as knowledgeable, authentic, and interesting.

One must note then that the Drunk and his cohorts did their homework. If the Drunk had approached the commuters soberly and, in a suit and tie, he probably would have been seen as just another salesman and stood the chance of being ignored. Had he been a regular drunk, without the eloquence, he would certainly be ignored. If he came as he did, but without the endorsement of the elderly Caucasian man, he would not have had any credibility and probably would have been ignored as well, and so the Drunk and those in collusion had to be forward thinking to properly execute their method of deception to win the crowd.

How then can one win when judging or not judging the book by the cover? How can a person discern the authentic amongst the inauthentic or camouflaged? The catch to this is the flip side, which is, if the intuition that raised the doubt was without prejudice and came from a place of sincerity, it has its merits, and almost always reveal an element of truth that supports the doubt.

Saying that to say, it would not be easy to see that the two men at the center of the Jasmine's encounter were performers, both of whom were creating a base to lure the inquisitive and vulnerable—seeking customers to build their clientele. It would not be easy to see that they were players of a long game, players who would win the trust of their audience and the contents of their wallets and pocketbooks overtime. Like the winners in the three-card game on the street corner, majority of the enthusiastic onlookers were indeed in collusion with the Ugly Drunk. Therefore, the anecdote's protagonist's doubt, though not taken seriously, was worth exploring.

One should be careful to note then, that counterfeit will always parade the identity and distinctiveness of the authentic to appear real. And, only the discerning, meticulous mind, and the refined apparatus can distinguish between the two.

...

One will agree that the factors of Jasmine's encounter with the Ugly Drunk is not unique. People deceive and rob people every day. Con artists and scammers are serious about their trade as though conning people is a legitimate venture. And, wolves will always take pleasure in wearing sheep's clothing to decimate flocks.

None of the deceivers mentioned will reveal their true nature; they will almost always approach with a lie that looks or sounds like the truth and they will almost always present good, when their inner works are evil.

In that regard—though many might deny—it is a fact that wrong and right, good and evil, truth and lie, have amalgamated into an unholy union that has changed the definition and distinctiveness of their respective "black" and "white" into cloudy-gray over time. Hence, truth is no longer seen by the masses as a constant, neither is wrong condemned. Hence, there is a constant battle between wrong and right, good and evil, as well as truth and lie, and though the battle—soaked in the subtle craft of deceit—is not acknowledged by the masses, it does not take away from the fact that there is a raging war going on between these entities.

...

When I was growing up, my grandmother usually used proverbs and folklore to warn me of the deceptions of indiscernible evils of the world. She once told me this story about Truth and Lie: the story says that, *Truth took off his garments and went down into the river for a bath. Lie, on the other hand, was passing by and saw Truth's garments on the riverbank. He took off his clothing and exchanged them for Truth's garments and went to town to flex his muscles. Many of the town folks looked admiringly at Lie and spoke of his truthful demeanor and close resemblance to Truth. Some were even convinced that Lie was Truth incarnate and they celebrated him. However, when Truth came out of the water and saw that his garments were missing, he refused to put on his rival's clothing; instead, Truth went to town naked. Upon his arrival, all the town folks disregarded Lie and pointed towards Truth, saying, here comes the Naked Truth!*

As frivolous as the story of "Truth and Lie" appears, it has some worrisome questions and serious implications that might have influenced Jasmine's initial doubt in the anecdote above, but more concerningly, cast doubt on many historical narratives. And, in the context of the war of good and evil, the implications cast doubt on many inherited foundational aspects of spiritual beliefs which, as a result, give rise to diverse interpretations that affect the destiny and direction of humanity.

Some of the worrisome questions are as follows: Why would Truth need to take a bath? Does that mean that if truth is left unattended it would corrode overtime? Does truth need regeneration or a constant voice to refresh and maintain its identity? Is truth identifiable to the masses amidst theatrics?

Why would Lie need Truth's clothing to go out and flex its muscles? How much overcoating does a lie needs to look like the truth? These questions do not exhaust all the possibilities, they simply lead to other questions, some of which are as follows: What is truth? Can truth be measured, proven, or replicated? Is truth confined to culture, or personal conviction?

To an extent, good and evil and right and wrong can be determined according to morals and ethics, culture, and the rule of law in a particular region, but there is an absoluteness to truth and lie that is supposed to be constant and universal but appears otherwise, undefined.

Many speaks of the relativity of truth, but one should note that it is a common fact that in every discipline knowledge increases, and the attitude towards the interpretation of these new information changes overtime as they are discovered, but that does not mean that there are degrees to truth, or that the truth has improved. Truth is always there. New findings only mean that man has made new discoveries.

...

The question then is, when did this union or marriage of good and evil take place and why should a person care about its implications? Here is when it took place: the marriage which resulted in the blurring of the lines of good and evil and or of wrong and right is not a trivial chance encounter that took place overnight. It is as old as dirt—designed with purpose and intentionality and took place when Lucifer and his host fell from heaven into the earth.

Here is why everyone should care: The marriage of the entities is a declaration of war against God himself. It is also a war against humanity. It is the same war that caused Jesus to come and die so that mankind could live. The same war in which the scripture says, that if the righteous scarcely be saved, where shall the ungodly and the sinner appear? The same war that caused the prophet Isaiah to say that the people are gone into captivity because they have no knowledge and as a result hell has enlarged herself and opened her mouth wide without measure. This war started in heaven when Lucifer wanted to raise his throne above the stars of God; when he campaigned for power, engaged in a coup-like war in which he was kicked out of heaven into the earth—which led to the desecration of the earth (Isa.14v12-17, Rev 12: 7-8).

As a result of Lucifer's fall, every natural entity has been tarnished and are directly attached to an "If, Then" structure or a reward and punishment type of spiritual premise. In this, according to the scriptures, it became Lucifer's plan to use trickery and ambiguity to cast a shadow on the things of God so as to create vagueness and doubt, to lure away even the strong, in order to win souls for his kingdom.

In this regard, to manipulate humanity, Lucifer simply mimics the systems of God, add a slight twist, and then use it to his advantage. A simple addition of a word to God's words bends and drastically alters the original and allows for several erroneous interpretations. Hence, the devil keeps the form so that it has less of an immoral tone and more of a logical appeal. Note though, that whatever the devil has modified, added to, or twisted, though it may seem logical, it has become a lie, dead works, and an evil vice.

...

In Lucifer's desperate bid to turn the black and white into cloudy gray, in order to create ambiguity so that he might confuse and mislead through counterfeit and deception, he imitates every structural pattern of Christ's government and Lordship.

For example, in heaven, there are angels with rank and appointment in similar manner as soldiers in armies of the world have rank and appointment. In the book of Colossians, a snippet of the celestial hierarchy, or ranking of angels are highlighted. This ranking consists of the following: Thrones, Dominions, Principalities, and Powers (Col. 1:16).

These four ranks that are named above do not exhaust the hierarchy of angels—the New Oxford American Dictionary describe Thrones as the third highest order of a ninefold celestial hierarchy.

In contrast, the devil also has a hierarchy of fallen angels that somewhat resembles the hierarchy described in Colossians consisting of the following: Principalities, Powers, Rulers of darkness of this world, and Spiritual Wickedness in high places (Eph. 6:12).

Here, in each group, the hierarchy of angels have principalities and powers in common—this can be accounted for due to the fact that a third of the angels in heaven were cast out in Lucifer's rebellion.

This kind of duplication or similarity continues, in that, Jesus is depicted as The Lion of the tribe of Judah. Here, like a foil character, the devil is characterized as a Roaring Lion, seeking whom he may devour (1 Peter 5:8).

Jesus is mentioned as the "Light of the World," and, in a similar sense, the devil is known to have the ability to make appearances like an angel of light (2 Corr. 11:14).

It is also worthy to note that at the end of the age, or in the great tribulation, the devil, in the antichrist, will declare himself as God, demonstrating signs and lying wonders.

In the above scenarios, the patterns of evil mimics the structural patterns of good, in the same manner that lie takes on qualities of truth.

Here, Lucifer has a spiritual structure that resembles the heavenly organization, his character mimics Christ's character as a roaring lion, he can take on qualities of angels of light in his appearances, and at the end of the age he will present himself as though he is God.

This axis of evil runs simultaneously with all of God's structural patterns intended to fog the distinctions of righteousness. But what is more troublesome, is the fact that one-third of the angelic host that fell from heaven in Lucifer's rebellion, those that are not otherwise bound, are involved in this dilemma—a host that is comprised of rank and authority with an agenda to deceive and mislead humanity.

...

Throughout time, the prophets warn, and preachers deliver messages about the dangers of this subtle deception of evil, yet to date, it appears the smog still fills the land.

Jesus knew that the believers would have this battle of distinguishing that which is deceptive from that which is authentic and so he gave us a clue which said, 'by the fruit you shall know them' and later he added a message of finality concerning the treacherous marriage of good and evil by saying, 'Let the wheat and the tares grow together until the day of harvest.'

The wheat and the tares are synonymous with or is a resemblance of the blurring of lines that took place with the two spiritual forces that operate in this world. That is, the force that promotes good and that which promotes evil—the two having no relationship between each other. Evil wars against good, and believe it or not, if you are not on the good side, your dwelling place is with evil.

...

It is a common thought, and rightly so, that for people to know where they are going, they need to know where they are coming from and what transport got them to where they are presently at.

But let's be honest. What would one do if at his or her disposal were the scrolls of old, the interpretation of the languages, and an angel as a tutor? Would that person's belief system be impacted? I think not. Regardless of the sources we have, there will always be a great disparity between generations concerning spiritual beliefs and of the transition, interpretation, and assimilation of the same.

Most of the inherited information will always be regarded as myths. Probably because there might not be enough physical evidence from generation to generation. But truth be told, if our present generation had the physical evidence that the preceding generations spoke of, I think we still would not believe it. Probably because one generation is more scientifically inclined than the other, the latter believe there should be solid and measurable evidence instead of faith.

For example, we read of Joshua in the scriptures where he commanded the sun to stand still, and we read of Moses' parting the red sea. If those phenomena should occur in our time, we would probably find some scientific explanation for them. As for Joshua commanding the sun to stand still which resulted into the longest day, we would probably say that there was a glitch in the solar system that happen every two billion years and caused the planets to temporarily stop their rotation, or maybe we would call it "summer solstice" but neither Joshua nor God would be credited. As for Moses, we would probably say that the separation of the waters at the red sea is a form of "allopatric speciation" of the Egyptian and the Jews. In any event, each generation refutes the preceding generation and fathers of faith, criticizing them and their legacy as erroneous. Thus, the trodden, proved, and paved path is rejected and the absurd is established.

Of course, knowledge has increased as stated earlier and of course we cannot live in the past. If we lived in the past, we would still believe that it is possible to fall off the edges of the earth and that the earth is not round. However, while we cannot live in the past, it is noteworthy to suggest that it's our history that defines us. Therefore, while we explore and build on valid ideas, we must be cognizant of exactly how we are building and make an extra effort to procure and preserve truth, because it's a sad thing when we as a nation begins to celebrate demons in theatrics, and deem their reality as inconspicuous, while righteousness and Godly wisdom are considered irrelevant. When this situation arises, it is time to take stock.

Generational shifts take place throughout civilization and knowledge increases from generation to generation, but there are certain foundational principles that should never be changed.

Note though that the foundational principles do not change with a bang, it is done without notice, as in a gentle drift. And, it usually start with inclusion, acceptance, and political correctness.

...

If you are old enough to remember, you will remember that there was a time when the term deadhouse drove fear into young children; nowadays, children do not even know what a deadhouse is. Deadhouse was previously referred to as parlor and from parlor, to morgue, to funeral home—which is more refined. The change in the terms desensitizes the effect and practically took away the fear that the term deadhouse once established—nobody wants to hear that his or her loved one is in a deadhouse.

If you are old enough to remember, you will remember that there was a time when men had to hide and watch pornography, it was considered a shameful act, but as time went by, the name changed to adult entertainment, and it became more accepting to the masses—and the once shamefaced men are now seen as macho.

If you are old enough to remember, you will remember that jailhouses and prisons had a devastating connotation that drove fear into delinquents, they are now called correctional facilities which sounds like a place for rehabilitation.

If you are old enough to remember, you will remember that drug addicts were once referred to as drug addicts and the term elicited pity and wonderment towards those involved; nowadays, addicts are seen as chemically dependent and the affected are seen as normal.

If you are old enough to remember, you will remember that there was a time when lazy students were called lazy students and parents and teachers would take measures to avert that laziness, but now they are considered unmotivated, and it becomes the teachers' fault.

If you are old enough to remember, you would recall that Afghanistan was referred to as the "graveyard of empires" for obvious reasons, armies always get bogged down in the chaos that goes on there, and almost always have to leave without achieving the required objective; yet none that left ever said that they were defeated when they were forced to leave. The military people would always say it was a strategic withdrawal, instead of using the term defeat or retreat—taking out the fear and dread or probably the shame that they have succumbed.

These politically correct terms are simply deceitful in the truest sense because the terms hide the true meaning and intensity in the language. The use of these euphemisms lessens the impact of words that perceived as harsh and insensitive in order to be politically correct, and to protect the feeling of others.

It is because of this word pollution, because of this sleight of hand, because of this marriage of good and evil, God stressed the importance of the law and told the children of Israel to write the laws as frontlets on their foreheads and tell it to their children. He then he gave them tables of stone, and afterwards he wrote upon the tables of their hearts—because he knew that there would be a generation that knows not the Lord.

...

Satan has been around for a while, and he understands the operation of the earthly realm. His works suggest that he never takes his eyes off the goal, which is to destroy humanity. He is determined to derail mankind from the purposes of God and hinder the intended destiny of humanity as he has done in Eden.

Satan knows quite well that there is a built-in vacuum inside of man that yearns to worship that which is of the greater appeal to the soul. He is also aware that the bearing of this appeal should be directed to God because man was created to worship God, so he must walk the tight rope and play the hand that he was dealt meticulously to get men to worship him. This is where his ingenuity kicks in. His cunning crafts must be impeccable and hard to detect and for the most part, excessively captivating because he knows fully well that he cannot approach humans directly with evil to attain worship.

Therefore, he must persuasively sell himself, and to do that, he must first initiate the grey area by blurring the lines. He must first inspire doubt in the midst of knowledge, fear instead of faith, and pleasure for the eyes that are vain. As the father of lies, he must put on truths garments and deceive the crowd to win the hearts of some.

It is in this regard that the continued battle is raging, and all the inhabitants of the earth are now involved, and the battle's momentum escalates as the end time approaches. For when the devil and his angels were cast out of heaven into the earth, they did not enter exile, neither did they rest, but proceeded to further establish dominion within the systems of the world. Therefore, the devil and his host constitute an enormous multitude, which is organized in a highly systemized and strategize empire of evil, with rank and order, having the world as their playing field. They are filled with malicious hatred and grudging envy, having prior knowledge of eternal defeat, rage a desperate war against anything that pertains to God.

I propose then, that to save the next generations and bring clarity to the present, we need to solicit campaigns as will the proceedings of this book, to unveil the mask of evil amongst us.

I propose that we safeguard truth in our homes and sphere of influence—calling a spade a spade and denounce evil.

I further propose that we, as the people of God, teach our children that not all that is politically correct, is right; not because congress pass laws means that it is expedient, we can be in the world and be not of the world.

I propose that as Christian Soldiers we train the Jasmines of our families to become discerners of the authentic, so that they might disregard the counterfeit and theatrics at first glance.

In the following chapters let us examine the armies of the

world as a module and use it as a launching pad in its physical state and in a psycho-spiritual sense to depict the enemy in the three dimensions, then compare it with the kingdom of God. This will give us a vivid picture to which we can relate, and when understood, we will appreciate the knowledge of what we are up against, and how to better arm ourselves against the wiles of the devil and establish our God given purposes in the earth.

Be sober, be vigilant; because your adversary the devil, as a roaring lion, walketh about, seeking whom he may devour.

1 Peter 5:8

Chapter Two
Evil Forces in Land, Sea, and Air

"What are you doing on New Year's Eve, Jasmine?" one of my colleagues asked.
"Um, I'm not sure. Why'd you ask?"
"A few of us are ringing in the New Year in the city, at the Oasis Restaurant, if you care to join."
It was an invite that most of my colleagues accepted. I committed to it because it came at a time when I was at my lowest. A time when I sought the company of any and everyone to replace the boredom and mild depression that was setting in. Some said the feeling was brought on by the change in the weather, others believed it came with the early darkness that descended at the end of daylight-saving time, but I somewhat believed it was the monotonous drag of the lonesomeness of study, blended with anxiety.
Against my better judgement—and my mother's wishes—I decided to skip the yearly ritual of ringing in the New Year with family and return to New York, to ring in the New Year.
I was not a fan of the setting at the Oasis. The sunny décor, cheerful and brilliantly colored vinyl booths gave me nostalgic anxiety and elicited bittersweet memories that I would rather suppress, and so that place was at the lower end of my palate. Nevertheless, the Jamaican Chinese cuisine that Chef Davi promoted, hit differently, it had a spicy kick that gave life to my taste buds and made me drool like a hungry pup. Truth be told, I went there for the food, and not so much for the conversation, but found myself at the bar mixing drinks and mingling in conversations I had no business getting

involved in.

The Oasis watering hole had the good, the bad, and the indifferent under one roof that evening. The slender faced Air Force captain in uniform stared at me as if I owed him money and had just bought myself a new car. His demeanor transformed and his slender face broke into a dimpled smile when I asked him what poison he was having.

He was drinking like a fish.

It was as if he were drinking his sorrows away. The talkative lawyer in the middle of the bar never gave his companions a chance to put in an idle word, his needless use of rhetoric and courthouse verbiage was overbearing; he cross-questioned and deliberated on simple subjects as though he were defending a high-ranking member of a drug cartel, and his life depended on his win. The nonchalant seaman to whom he directed most of his arguments, had a curse-word for every rebuttal. It was as though their masculine egos bumped into each other and sucked the oxygen from the room—everyone wanted to tell his story.

I scanned the room further. People from all classes, creed, and culture were present. To my surprise, even a couple of my professors were there. I greeted a few of my colleagues and chatted with them a little, but I was more drawn to the quiet fellow at the end of the bar who seemed as though he was out of place. Either he had the magnetic pull, or I did, but I was drawn to him. It is said that misery likes company. He was obviously miserable, and I chose to be his company. I learned later, through our conversation, that he was a soldier, about to be deployed for his second tour in Afghanistan in the coming days.

I flirted with him and he with me. For a moment, it seemed as though I was the analgesic to his pain. His militant mood mellowed, and his mystified demeanor lightened like sunshine from ominous clouds with every passing moment. He transformed from a glum to a conversationalist.

He mocked my Mimosa and introduced me to the Incredible Hulk. Halfway through the first glass of this green elixir, I felt as though I had too much to drink.

Chef Davi came over and presumably asked if I had tried his special. I saw his mouth moving, but all I heard was the word special. I was now certain that I drank too much. Or had I? As my recollection serves, I knew I drank much more than this in the past and was able to drive.

Tonight, after my second glass, involuntary muscles tingled and throbbed, and I felt somewhat dazed as a strange feeling of longing for human embrace swept over my body. I felt vulnerable, but at ease. I was in the company of intellectuals and professionals— Seaman, Air Force captain, and even lawyers. Therefore, I felt safe. But, I also knew it was time to leave before I embarrassed myself. I decided against calling an Uber, thinking that standing in the cold to flag a cab would revive me faster. I promised myself that next year I would be in a better condition to ring in the New Year.

Without saying my goodbyes, I slipped on my coat, clutched my purse, and stepped off unsteadily. I felt the powerful arm of my transformed conversationalist as he steadied me before offering me a ride. I was in no position to refuse. But I did. Nevertheless, my legs would not play the role they were created for. I beckoned to one of my colleagues and she came over—laughing at my seemingly wasted condition, asking if it wasn't too early for me to be drunk.

My mind was conscious but was incongruent with the sluggish movements of my limbs. My female colleague had seen me in conversation with the soldier at the bar earlier, and I supposed she thought it was okay for him to take me home and so she gave in to his eager appeal of doing me the honors.

As we went towards the door, I wasn't sure if it was a fist bump, or a handshake one of my professors gave the soldier, but it made me uncomfortable. I never saw them speaking throughout the evening, and I had no knowledge if they had met prior. And so, I became paranoid. I wasn't sure if I was a part of a game, or it was a sincere greeting; therefore, in my mind I was pulling back with every inch of my strength. But the heavy feeling in my stomach and the lethargic feeling in my legs was no match to the strong arms of the soldier who by this time held my arm over his shoulder and his other hand on my hip.

He walked me almost a quarter of a block to his car. The crisp wind blowing into our faces. When we got to the car, I reached for the passenger seat door, but he swirled me about and opened the rear door of the car and literally stuffed me in. Feeling a bit nauseated, I rolled the window halfway down to let the air in. The wind bash against my face and ravished my hair.

"10—," I said, giving just the apartment number of my address. "Turn around right here. The other way." I said again, as I noticed him going in the wrong direction. "You are going…" I heard the locks click on the car door. Instinctively, I heaved forward, slumped, and heaved. Grabbed his shoulder and pulled him back from the steering. The car swerved almost out of control as he slowed, turned, and parked on the side of the road.

"Why the commotion?" he asked.

"Where in hell are you taking me?" I screamed.

"I am taking you home, isn't that where you want to go?" came his unperturbed response.

"You don't even know my address!"

He switched off the engine, sprang from the car, and before I could get out, he was beside me on the back seat. I reached for the door; he clicked the locks shut and shoved the keys into his pockets. Then, without words or warning, he reached down, grabbed, and dragged my legs towards him, pushed them up in the roof of the car and got me on my back, almost breaking my neck in the process. Never in my life have I ever encountered someone with such enormous strength. In that confinement, my body was flung about from side to side like a ragged doll.

I could not fight this monstrous assailant; I could not match him pound for pound, but I wasn't going to go down without a fight. He'd have to kill me before he violated me further. I punched, scratched, and screamed. He grunted, grabbed, guffawed, and pushed my hand under me and held it there. He was now between my legs—one curled in under him and the other over his shoulder.

In that moment, I pushed my free hand down my throat and induced vomit—spitting all over him, but he never flinched. He pulled his belt with his free hand and reached beneath my already-up skirt pulling down my spandex. With my free hand I tried to block his attempt from pulling it down. I twisted from side to side and screamed. Hoping that someone would hear me through the half-opened window. With each passing moment I was regaining strength and clarity of mind. I screamed louder and louder. He pinned me down with his body, then paused, pulled out a rag and attempted to stuff it down my throat. I sunk my teeth into his hand, and he dragged it from my mouth and punched me in the face.

My free hand bumped into my purse, and I rummaged for the pocketknife inside of it. My hand landed on the knife, but I could not open the blade with one hand, so I butted him in the face with the knife. He released my arm and grabbed and compressed my throat with both of his hands. I was sucking for oxygen that was not coming. I tried to hit him again. He pushed down harder on my throat. I was losing the fight. The strength that I had regained from the air in my face and the looseness of my stomach after I vomited was gone.

And, I knew my time had come. I was out of options and almost out of breath. The thought of my mother pleading for me to stay flashed across my mind.

If only I had stayed.

Tears flooded my eyes. I gagged, almost unconscious. In that moment, I saw the silhouette of a man with his hand going up and down as what seemed like a baseball bat crashed into the window on the other side. I sucked for air as my assailant released my neck and turned around towards the interruption.

A flurry of curse words ensued. The advancement of clattering feet could be heard. The baseball bat pounded the window again. The glass caved. My assailant alighted from the car in a furious rage and confronted the rescuer. I reached for the door lock, opened and dragged myself to the outside, falling on the hard pavement. My assailant got into an altercation with my rescuer and a tussle ensued. More clattering feet approached. I raised myself up on my elbows, then uncomfortably on the side of my arm and watched. I small crowd had gathered. My assailant rushed to the front door, opened, and took what I realized was a gun from the glove compartment. He pushed it into the retreating rescuer's face and in between a flurry of expletives, he said, "Sleep on the same side you slept last night, because tonight is your lucky night!" The rescuer and the small crowd that had gathered, backed up. My assailant came around to the passenger's side of the car, walked casually towards me, looked down, stepped on my wrist as though it was just a piece of debris on the ground, held my gaze, then casually walked back to the driver's door, got in the car, and drove away.

A few cars slowed and stopped, lights shining in my face. I heard the sirens and saw the flashing lights.

The last thing I saw as I laid there on the cold concrete before waking up in the hospital, was a man, about five feet eleven inches, standing over me with a baseball bat over his shoulder, wearing pearly white sneakers with bright red streaks, asking me if I would be okay. The ambulance attendants and the police were asking him to step aside for a moment. I looked at him a second time; his face briefly became familiar, then it blurred. It was the Ugly Drunk.

If we should take certain aspects of Jasmine's encounter into consideration, we would realize that though her company that evening was filled with intellectuals and people of considerable affluence and status, the group was not excluded from the dangers of the degenerate mindset. It is also worthy to note that the person who was expected to protect her from all evils, foreign and domestic, was the actual evil that she needed to be protected from. And, the hoodlum, or the "Ugly Drunk" who she had previously seen on the train—the same scoundrel who made it his business to scam and deceive, was the savior that came to her rescue.

The anecdote can be seen then as an example of the fallibility that plague humanity. It is not that we are all wolves in sheep's clothing, instead, it is a stark reminder that in the best of us there is the propensity to do evil and in the worst of us there is the capacity to do good.

The common factor in having the capacity to do good, the propensity for entertaining evil can be seen in the cataclysmic occurrence of Jasmine's encounter; that common factor, was people. This tells us then that evil spirits need the minds and bodies of people to operate effectively. This also means that, for demonic strong-holds and presence to be established in the land, the sea, or in the air, people have to yield their minds and their will to the devils.

Note then, that the devil operates in every strata of society and takes residence among the good, the bad, and the indifferent.

Hence, the devil uses powerful people in high authority the same way he uses the delinquents who dwell in the gutters.

When the Bible states that *we wrestle not against flesh and blood but against principalities, against powers, against the rulers of darkness of this world, against spiritual wickedness in high places*, it does not take away the involvement of people. It is merely enforcing the idea that there is a driving force behind the actions of people. People must be overtaken by a fault for demons to have preeminence or create strongholds. Whatever the fault is, it could be greed, malice, grudge, pride, or lusts, you name it, it does not matter, people must be present for demons to act efficiently in the earth.

It is a misconception to believe that demonic presence only exists in forms of witchcraft. This is war. The devils infiltrate society through every social ills that plagues humanity, whether it be through—racism, forms of enslavement, marginalization, biases, discrimination, or even as high as the powers who exploit or exert control over sovereignty other than their own. The bottom line is that there is a spiritual connection to every good and evil operation.

...

I promised in the previous chapter that I would use the armies of the world in their physical state, and in a spiritual sense, to depict the enemy in the three dimensions so here goes—

Everywhere that Lucifer and his angels fell when they got kicked out of heaven has become a war zone. Hence, the war rages in the land, on the sea, and in the air.

The Bible records the sons of God presenting themselves before him. In that meeting, the devil also presented himself among the sons of God. And, when he was asked, from whence he came, he replied, *'From going to and fro in the earth, and from walking up and down in it'* (Job 2:1-2).

In the same manner that this spiritual scenario depicts the whereabouts of the devil, there is also a physical resemblance in the land.

Whether or not people take the answer to that question seriously, that answer was God inspired. God already knew where the devil was, he simply wanted us to know. That answer was a personal testimony from the devil himself—he is present in the earth, going to, and fro, walking up and down in it.

...

The security strength of any country is determined by the strength of that country's armed forces arsenal, leadership, manpower, as well as its international allegiances or counterparts. And, in the same manner that soldiers in the armies of the world are organized and strategically placed at key points all over their country, the devils and his emissaries saturate authorities and systems and strategizes themselves in and at key points of influence within the systems, trafficking to and fro.

...

When it comes to the evil occurrences on the sea, there are a plethora of references. The scripture records in the book of Genesis that darkness was upon the face of the deep. And, as we know, darkness is a scriptural representation of evil (Gen. 1:2). In the Genesis scenario, God had to give a command against the dark restraint, by saying, *'let there be light'* so that his perfect will might come to pass.

A commentary that gives vivid details of the dark forces that dwell on the sea was chronicled when Jesus and his disciples went on a ship and were going over to the other side into the land of the Gadarenes. The scripture records that Jesus fell asleep on the ship and the winds became tempestuous so much so that the roaring waves battered the vessel in which they traveled. The terrified disciples cried out in desperation to their peacefully, sleeping master and asked if he didn't care that they were about to perish. With that, he arose and rebuked the wind and there was a great calm.

It was not only that distress and intimidation were wrapped up in that tempestuous wind—revealing the insecurities and fears of the disciples; the text revealed too, that the wind, being tempestuous, was an obstruction to Jesus and the disciples' visit. And, in case that first checkpoint or deflection wasn't successful in deterring them, there was a secondary checkpoint, a barrier, put in place by fierce demons that possessed the individual who lived among the tombs—stationed there to obstruct the passageway of redemption.

Jesus asked the possessed young man his name, and he said, "Legion," because many devils had entered into him (Matt. 8 v 23-34, Mark 5:1-20). If you read that text in its entirety, you will notice that the people of the land they visited were not very accepting of Jesus. They did not welcome him; therefore, since the dark forces of the sea which was embodied in the tempestuous wind could not stop him, the spiritual connection of evil hindrances upon the borders of its shore—presented in the demon possessed—raged against him as soon as he and his disciples came off the sea.

This text then begs for the question—why? Why did Jesus and his disciples go through so much just to turn back at that point? The answer is simple—like the woman of Samaria, the man that was possessed by demons was chosen for a mission, the mission in which he ended up evangelizing the city after Jesus delivered him.

Saying all of this to say that there is a spirit that controls the activities of the seas. In our world a military presence is always on the sea. Whether it is sea-cadet, coastguard, or the navy, they dominate and control the activities of the sea.

Their purpose is often stated in a nice way as protecting and serving, but in fact, they are there to hinder, by any means necessary, any incongruency, or foreign objects that are of threat to their country or system of control.

...

With regards to the air, the Bible speaks of 'Spiritual Wickedness in high places' (Eph. 6:12). This could very well mean wickedness within high levels of leadership within the hierarchy of society, but from another point of view, Spiritual Wickedness in high places could be a direct, literal, reference to the devil, seeing that he is the 'Prince of the power of the air.' And, as such, can manipulate every manifestation that traffics in the air, whether it be angelic, human, mechanical entities, or media related material that travels on the airwaves.

The scriptures states that Daniel was going through a period of mourning, and he set his heart to understand the things of God, hence he sought the Lord through fasting, supplication, and prayers.

The scripture declares that from the first day that Daniel started praying, his prayers were heard, and an angel came for his prayer. But the Prince of the Kingdom of Persia withstood the angel for twenty-one days. It took Michael, one of the chief princes of the kingdom of God, to rush to that angel's aid, so that the angel could bring the answer and minister to Daniel (Daniel 10:13).

These devils never wanted Daniel to receive the answers and understanding that God had for him, so they tried every preventative measure to hinder it, even to stop the angel that was carrying the answers and revelations.

Therefore, it is clear that the war rages in the air, which compares with the defensive mechanism of the armies of the world, which lies within their air forces.

...

None of the dark forces in any of the dimensions mentioned above is meant to cause paranoia or scare anyone. Instead, it is presented for the awareness of the believer. The scripture states that the people of God perish because of lack of understanding.

Therefore, in order to be successful in a warfare, one must know the enemies' tactics and thereby know what to anticipate and how to maneuver.

Here is the understanding that the Christian soldier should have: Every man is made with purpose. Man was created in God's image and likeness. That means that man can speak as God spoke and cause things to happen. More importantly, since God gave Adam dominion over the fowl of the air, the fish of the sea, and over everything that creeps on the earth, that suggests that Adam had dominion over air, land, and sea, and everything that dwells therein.

In addition to man having dominion over all the dimensions that the devil is running rampant through, God gave man the power over every power of the devils. The believer was given power to bind kings with chains and nobles with fetters of iron. That means, mankind has authority and dominion not only over physical embodiment, but also the spiritual realm and the entire body of intruders that appear to be in control.

As a Christian soldier in the believer's battle, it is fitting to ask the following question: what could Jasmine have done in her situation, and what was it that really saved her? Was it her agility and fighting skills? Was it the Ugly Drunk? Or was it her mother's prayers? Was it by chance that her mother was begging her to stay at the family function? As we progress through the chapters, we will examine these aspects particularly when dealing with the benefits of the armor of God.

Chapter Three
Spiritual and Physical Fundamentals

Escaping the hangman's noose provided me the opportunity to reflect and introspect. As I lay there trembling in the hospital bed, a jet stream of every imaginable 'what ifs, ands/ buts' of what could have happened, and how I could have avoided the entire scenario invaded my mind. I thought too, about the pains my mother would have felt if I was sexually assaulted that night. The daily guilt she might have felt knowing that maybe, just maybe, if she had begged me more to stay, I probably would have, as I did at other times when she annoyingly persuaded me.

But more importantly, when my stomach was pumped and I later learned that traces of ketamine—a date rape drug—was found in my system, I thought about the shame I would have felt, the deep abhorrence I would have carried for the opposite sex, and the relapse of pain and suffering with each wave of memory, if my assailant was successful.

In the absence of a father figure in our home, my mother never missed an opportunity to teach me how to circumvent the guile of men—to the point that I somewhat engendered a bit of fear of falling prey to a male chauvinistic community even as a small child. But now, it was as though my greatest fear had almost overtaken me. I felt sick to the stomach as I wondered how many more victims had succumbed to this ordeal at the hand of my assailant

The doctor checked in once more and told me that she held me overnight for observation and other preliminaries since I had an episode of blocking out, but that I would be discharged soon. The police officers came and took their report—or whatever that was called. Though they spoke softly, they probed me in a manner that felt as if I was being mildly interrogated. Asking me the time I got to the restaurant and the time I left. Asking me how long I knew the fellow. Asking me if it was a misunderstanding. Asking me if I suggested or initiated sex. Asking me how much drinks I had. Asking me why I didn't ask one of my girlfriends for a ride. Asking me why I didn't call a cab. Asking me if he forced me into his car or if I entered freely. I answered the questions a bit less than cordially, through clenched teeth, anticipating the end.

It was obvious that my next of kin was notified—because my mother was standing over me the whole time. Nevertheless, through it all, my entire headspace was in disarray. My mother stepped out and went to get coffee as the Attending Nurse reentered the room.

The Attending Nurse looked at me with what I perceived to be wide-eyed-pity, but what I later learned were anxiety and fear. She was a nervous wreck—probably more nervous than I was. She stuttered at my questions and answered cautiously with trembling lips. And, in her bid to show compassion or give comfort, propped up my bed without me asking, poured me water, and held onto my hand unusually long, telling me it was going to be okay. Her dangling identification card necklace fell from behind her blouse when she bent to prop up the bed, and I caught sight of the pictured sonogram at the back. My eyes naturally went to her flat stomach.

"Congratulations," I said, pointing at her necklace, conjuring up the best possible smile I could, "how far along are you?" I asked softly, almost in a whisper. She smiled nervously with trembling lips, replaced the identification card in her bosom, and held on to my hand. I held her gaze, and for a moment, I studied her eyes. The deep misery and pain they held became apparent.

"This might not be a good time," her voice breaking as she cleared her throat.

"It's fine, um, sorry," I said, apologetically. She smiled sheepishly without answering.

In that moment, the vibration in my pocketbook arrested my attention and I reached over the nearby stand, grabbed the pocketbook, and shuffled for my phone. The vibration stopped abruptly. When I took out the phone, I noticed a slew of missed calls, and a low battery signal. "Can I borrow an iPhone charger of some sorts? My phone is almost dead," she left the room as though she never heard my request but returned momentarily with a charger. I nodded in appreciation and told her thanks.

"Three years ago, at this time, I was in your position. Only, I wasn't as lucky," I heard her say as I looked up from the phone. She was holding onto the identification cardholder—the sonogram facing me. "It's not always the ones that we'd expect, but those that communicate with us—the ones with whom we let down our guard and become comfortable."

"Hmm."

"Yes, I know I wasn't supposed to hear the testimony that you gave to the police. Nevertheless, I never had the chance to fight as I heard you did, in your testimony. I was out, cold. When I woke up, I had flashes of disjointed memories, heaviness in the stomach, lethargic and nauseating feelings—the same feeling you'd probably have felt after a hangover," she turned, pulled the curtains, and looked outside. "My incident wasn't reported either," she turned and faced me. "I woke up in my own bed. And, the man was not present. Sometimes, out of self-pity, I told myself it was a shameful one-night stand, but in reality, I don't remember inviting him in my home after he dropped me off."

"Oh, no, I am so sorry."

"It's okay," she answered and paused. The deafening silence and awkward moments filled the spaces between glances of pity, repugnance, and gratefulness.

"What gender?" I asked, trying to validate my doubts as to why she modeled the sonogram instead of her child if her incident was three years ago. This time, she turned the sonogram to herself.

"I was too ashamed of what might transpire if I reported the crime. The eventualities of my convictions prevented me—or probably my naivety and ignorance at the time. I wrestled with my convictions even before my missed cycle and the sonogram confirmed my intuition. Being religious, I battled against the relics of tradition that my family and my church upheld. And, being free from them, am now trapped in a prison of guilt, regrets, embarrassment, and shame—I mean, what if I had kept the child, would she have been the child of a criminal? And who am I to ask that question, knowing that I am responsible for denying her a chance at life?"

She released the key chain, pursed her lips, held her head between her palms and shook her head from side to side. I was shocked at the level of her vulnerability. And, being unable to find the right words, I said the best thing I knew.

"It's...it's not your fault," I stammered, sitting up in the bed, making myself an active listener, "you are not to be blamed, and you cannot blame yourself for the evils of another. You didn't do it to yourself, you have been victimized. And, you cannot remain a victim either." I heard myself rattling off words, sounding like my mother—giving unsolicited advice amidst consolation. I quickly got myself together, stopped talking, and nervously reflected on my probably unwanted outburst. But she appeared deeply distanced, as her gathered tears rolled down her plump cheeks. I arose from the bed, stepped closer, hugged, and held her for a moment. I could feel her tense muscles relax as she returned the embrace. She felt as if she was a sister in my arms—or that next of kin that one would have gone to prison for. That person who you would never leave to fight on his or her own. "The painful memories won't go unless you let them," I said, reassuringly, "you have to let it go."

In that moment, it felt as though I was giving away the resuscitative embrace and healing vernacular that I needed for myself, at a time I needed them most. At the same time, it was as though I was speaking to myself, because the reverberation in the tone of my voice rebounded like a boomerang in my head, creating a therapeutic sensation that administered peace to my troubled mind and made me feel at ease.

What passed between us in that moment, was an electrifying human experience of trust, vulnerability, and the need for each other.

My mother reentered the room. About an hour and a half or two later, I was released from the hospital. Before I left, I made it my duty to inquire for my Attending Nurse. To my surprise, she was not wearing her keychain; instead, her identification card was clipped onto her blouse.

I smiled broadly at her.

"I destroyed it," she said, pointing to the new identification card holder. "I had to let it go."

I was mildly ecstatic. In the few moments that we shared, it felt as though we had created a bond, released a weight, and rescinded the elements of a destructive path.

Train up a child in the way he should go, and when he is old he will not depart from it.

Proverbs 22:6

There is a common factor in Jasmine's New Year's Eve encounter, and the experience of the Attending Nurse. That common factor is an open door. The door in Jasmine's life was her fear of falling prey to the guile of a male chauvinistic community—which, by the way, had almost overtaken her; while the door in the Attending Nurse's life, though not explicitly stated, resulted in her being violated and then tagged with the guilt and shame symbolized by the picture in the sonogram that tied and imprisoned her to the memory.

The doors in these characters' lives were not created during their adult lives. Doors are almost always created during the innocent stages of children, and if left unchecked, provide entrance for devils in the later years. In essence, doors are opened and closed through lifestyle principles and practices. For this cause, the scripture admonishes the believer to train up children in the way they should go, so that when they are old, they will not depart from it (Prov 22:6).

But why do godly parents place emphasis on the need to train the new members of the family—speaking of little children? Why not let them be what they are called, children? The answer to that is quite simple: foolishness is wrapped up in the hearts of children; as a result, they become prime targets for devils, so much so, that, if left unchecked, the once cute, unrighteous machinations that children practice in their youth, will develop into permanent evils that will metastasize like cancerous tumors in the later years;

hence, as long as they are children, they need to be under tutors and governors so they can be trained in the way that they should go (Gal 4:2).

Another reason children are prime targets for devils is that children are a heritage of the Lord—and the fruit of the womb, is his reward (Ps. 127 :3). On this scripture hinges a major motivation why the devils hate children with the vehement passion that they do. In that, if it is God's pride and joy to bless families with children, then it becomes the devil's desire to destroy the blessings of God; as a result, the children—if not protected and trained—becomes susceptible to the exploits of devils.

Think about the fact that when Jesus was a child, his parents had to run away with him to Egypt so that the devil, in Herod, wouldn't kill him. Moses' parents had to hide Moses in a basket on a river so that the devil, in Pharoah, would not kill him. Like Jesus and Moses, every child is born with a purpose, and the devil will always want to kill the child—literally and spiritually—so that the purpose would die in the process.

In one instance, Jesus had to rebuke his very own disciples and tell them to suffer the children to come unto him, for of such is the kingdom of God. And, to the adults, the message is clear, except adults become as children, they cannot enter the kingdom of God. Children signify strength and unity, continuity and permanency, generational growth and productivity, innocence and humility, love and loyalty, home and family. Therefore, any chance the devils get to shred them apart in their innocence, they spare no expense to do so—to ensure that they do not fulfill their God given purposes.

More importantly, if the devils cannot shred them in their tender years, the devils create doors in their lives—as in planting seeds of dysfunctionality in the system, the society, their immediate environment, in their homes, and within the families to ensure that the children are exposed and entrapped. This is one of the reasons psychotherapists will almost always question the childhood experiences of adults to uncover what door was opened and what was buried in the subconsciousness that might be a trigger to present conditions.

Note here that no earthly being is exempted from the eventuality of an open door. Once you are born, you are born in sin and shaped in iniquity—thus, doors are created.

Though Jesus was not earthly, he was not exempted from the warped systems of society and the propositions of an open door through a dysfunctional family. In that, a harlot was mentioned in his genealogy; hence, an environment conducive to sensuality and seduction was created—yet, that did not affect his tendencies. The scriptures stated that though he was tempted in all points, he was without sin (Heb 4:15).

Jesus' response to the scheme of an open door was, 'The prince of this world cometh, and hath nothing in me' (John 14:30). That means, the seeds that the devil planted did not germinate; therefore, the devil had no claim or authority over him—nothing in him belong to the devil. Nothing in the system, the society, or his environment was tied up in his spirit. He was not a sinner—he had no tendency to sin, which means that the doors that the devils set did not impact him.

...

Jesus did not leave us ignorant, he gave us the tools that would enable us to be successful amidst the treacherous eventualities of open doors in our lives, in systems, and in societies. The believer is equipped with tools that develop character trait, moral compass, code of conduct, and ethics. Those tools are wrapped in the fruits of the spirit and gifts of the spirit. Having these tools and proper training in the word of the Lord, the believer will be able to fortify foundations, create sustainable structures, build bulwarks of protection, and inspire children in a way that will impact their generation to become agents of change.

Parents are therefore advised to train up their children by teaching and leading them to study God's foundational principles and guidelines so that they might become disciplined and responsible, and by doing so, show themselves approved unto God. As were prescribed to the children of Israel, parents and guardians of the children of this generation should, figuratively, bind the words of the Lord as a sign on their hands, and keep them as frontlets between their eyes. Parents should teach the word of the Lord to their children every opportunity they get. When they sit down, rise up, or walk in the way—writing them upon the door posts of their houses so that everything might be well with them (Deu 11:18).

...

It is noteworthy to mention that in every viable organization, there are rules and regulations engrafted at the core to foster a firm structure to ascertain longevity or permanency. In that regard, to maintain the life of any successful organization, the continued enforcement of those ground rules and regulations must be replicated to ensure success—the preservation of these core values are established through training.

Creating structure and foundation by adhering to rules and regulations are not limited to large organizations or systems. To avoid chaos and breaches of any kind, everything in life must be done decently and in order.

In the same sense that there is a structure in every system of the body, there is supposed to be a structure in the foundation of the home and family. Even the very fast-food chain stores have structure—

Any disruption or foreign intrusion, any malfunction, or neglect, to any part of the structure, or the foundation of any system—small or great—that system will be opened to chaos and breaches and as a result, will be destroyed over time. To that, the scripture says, if the foundation be destroyed what can the righteous do? (Ps. 11:3).

In that regard, if the manager of a fast-food chain store hires a new employee, that manager does not concern him or herself with the amount of prior experience that that employee might have had, the employee must be retrained according to the system and standard of the new employment.

In similar sense, when an addition is made to a family, that child needs to be trained, streamlined, and cultured in order to be aligned and become compatible with the protocols or culture of that new family.

...

In this manner, the army is on point with regards to creating foundational structure against treacherous eventualities of open doors. And, since the scripture mention that one should endure hardship as a good soldier because no man that is engaged in warfare entangles himself with the affairs of this life, let us use the structure of the army to establish a viable pattern in the believer's battle (2Tim 3).

The structural foundation that is engrafted in the army can be seen in the chain of command and basic training of recruits. In the training of the army's recruits, there is a form of discipline, structure, and continuity that is worthy of emulating.

Their rank and files contain the Chiefs of Staff, who communicates with, and take orders directly from the security minister, or the head of the government, and that order is distributed down the ranks as necessary. Working with the chiefs of staff, are staff officers, who usually have committed duties related to the responsibilities of the chiefs on which they report directly to their hierarchy.

Then there are Generals, Colonels, Majors, Captains, Lieutenants, Warrant Officers, Sergeants, Corporals, Privates and Recruits. In these ranks and files, everyone is in total submission to his superior officer and are bound by their core values of commitment, integrity, loyalty, honesty, and discipline.

Rank and appointments are held in high esteem; in that, all the directives come from the top and goes down through the rank and files to the bottom, and no subordinate can refute his superior.

In this arena, recruits—like children in families—conform systematically and are vigorously trained in land, sea, and air maneuvers, to compliment the continued potency of the army's arsenal.

It is therefore a requirement that the recruits exhaust every required training standard at its peak before they graduate and blend into the rank and files of the soldiers. If a recruit fails to achieve and excel in this required endeavor, he or she is then 'back squad' (placed aside to retrain in the next intake).

A part of their training includes skills at arms, tactical training, hand-to-hand combat, watermanship, field craft, map reading, drills, and reaction to enemy forces. To explain a few, skills at arms is the ability to recognize, access and apply themselves spontaneous and effectively to weapons of all description and capability at any given moment with ease and versatility.

In tactical training, the recruits are taught how to master all arts of military maneuvers—characterized by personal skills and cleverness. In the same breath, combat training enables them to fight opponent or opposition in any struggle or battle, with and by any means necessary, to overthrow and or conquer.

Field craft, like water-man-ship, is the subtle craft of stealth to survive and manipulate without being noticed on land and water respectively.

Along with physical and mental training there are also psychological methods used to break the recruits from the civilian mentality to the military focus. And, this is done through songs, games, and prayers.

Let us take prayer as our example, and see how best it befits this occasion, as many are already exposed to war movies and understands the psychological intent of mock battle games and motivational songs.

The prayer of the recruit describes his proposed character, attitude and mannerism. This prayer must be prayed every mealtime and whenever called upon by an instructor to recite same. This is done with specific training methods until it mentally molds these individuals into weapons of war. One of the prayers is as follows: *'The infantry soldier's basic attitude must be that of a fighter for fighting sake. He must be unquestionably obedient and become emotionally hard. He must have the strongest bond of comradeship for those who do belong to the order, particularly his fellow soldiers. He must think nothing impossible. He is trained to kill.'*

Let's spend some time analyzing the recruit's prayer and see how the principle might benefit the believer, or children in the home and family.

The prayer lasts for the duration of training—which, initially, would be about six months. And, it must be said at every mealtime— which is at least three times a day. This means, the recruits regurgitated these lines at least five hundred and forty times before the completion of their initial training.

The repetition of the prayer was not for mere memorization or for emphasis; every single word was connected to the daily operation and was practiced in every aspect of their training. In that, as stated in their prayers, it was extremely pertinent that the recruits become emotionally hard. It was a necessity that they have the strongest bond of comradeship—and training to kill goes without saying, it was almost always expedient to their survival. By this, we know undoubtedly, that the recruits have been indoctrinated in such a way that their characters have been transformed by their prayer. In other words, they have become their prayer.

Hence, it is fair to say that the prayer of the recruit is unequivocally supreme to the rest of his training, in that, it embodies faith in his belief, unity with comrades, love for fellowmen, obedience to orders, and a fighting character that is stable minded and focused.

Note too, that the Recruit's basic attitude should be that of a fighter for fighting sake, which means that every inclination of his entire mental and physical state, should be in a position of impulsive readiness.

Incidentally, a soldier's training never ends. The old motto is that 'the more you sweat in training, the less you bleed in war'. Therefore, through blood, sweat, and tears, the recruits will embrace hardship, conquer stress, and endure pain. Recruits are trained to face their fears with determination and use endurance as a key ingredient to accomplish harder missions.

A robot of a man, with the heart of a lion, prepared and ready to fulfill every mission. Some usually run away from the training; there are times when some even die therein; but for the most part, the majority complete the initial training, injured and worn, knowing that that was only the beginning.

The high point of this, is that the recruits are trained to become unquestionably obedient and emotionally hard—this is to say, regardless of situations, irrespective of conditions, in spite of all cause, the recruit must and will stand at his post, in the line of duty, without thinking twice to execute his disposition.

As did the soldiers before them, the training is done so that when recruits graduate, they become a replica of their predecessors; in this regard, they are broken from the civilian mentality, their comrades have become family, and they are sworn to commitment and loyalty—marching to the same drumbeat as of the women and men in uniform who trained them. Every affinity to civilian lifestyle has been ripped from the core of their character and every idle door has been closed. Therefore, upon this premise of training, the structure and foundation of the army is built, and its continued potency is established.

...

In the same manner that there is a chain of command or hierarchal ladder in the army that is geared towards creating foundational structure against treacherous eventualities, God establishes his hierarchy in the heavens, and places representatives in the earth. For example, in heaven there are Archangels, Seraphim, Cherubim, Angels with authority, Dominion, and Ministering Spirits—all of whom are in charge of God's affairs and act according to his bidding.

The representatives in the earth are reflected in the fivefold ministry—which include the Apostles, Prophets, Evangelists, Pastors and Teachers. These appointments and appointees are geared towards the perfecting of the saints, the work of the ministry, and the edifying of the body of Christ (Eph 4:11-12).

In the work of the ministry, the positioning and purposes of these spirit filled leaders are as follows: Apostles are spirit-filled pioneers who manifest extraordinary leadership style directly confronting the powers of darkness, breaking grounds, and erecting new churches regardless of the volatility of the territory. In the New Testament the term was applied to those who have seen Christ and was originally appointed by him.

The prophets have a unique responsibility that sets them apart. The representatives in this role are like watchmen over the body of Christ, anointed to fearlessly pull down and destroy strongholds, to throw down and trample the powers of darkness, build up and to plant, exhorts, edify and comfort (Jer.1:5). Representatives in this role expose sin without prejudice, proclaim righteousness without apology, and with the adroitness of a seasoned orator, warns of judgment to come. These representatives usually have a deep sensitivity of the spiritual world a strong spirit of discernment.

The evangelists are anointed to proclaim the gospel of salvation to the unsaved; the main concern of these representatives is to see converts transformed and filled with the Holy Spirit; hence, winning souls for the Kingdom of God, and helping to establish new works in different pockets of the vineyard.

Teachers are those who God gave special gifts to clarify,

illustrate and unpack difficult scriptural premise into amicable uncompromising procedures to edify the body of Christ.

The pastors are the overseers, whose task is to proclaim sound doctrine and refute heresy, hence safeguarding apostolic truth. Pastors are very essential to God's purpose in the earth; in that, they must lead the people of God into uncompromising holiness.

Even though God is independent of all these representatives because of his attributes, (Omnipotent, Omnipresent, Omniscient, etc.,) pastors are held accountable for the souls of the church—therefore, as the under-shepherd, pastors are obligated to ensure that the people dwell into the divine grace of God. Hence, the pastor—and the representatives mentioned above—guided by the Holy Spirit, are bound by the rule of holiness unto the Lord, and to be blameless (1Tim 3).

The congregation that these leaders govern are the family of God—better known as the children of the Lord, the believers, or the saints. These include senior saints, the young in Christ, new converts (or recruits), as well as backsliders. The scripture is careful to admonish the congregation to be in total obedience to those who are set over them, since their promotion did not come from the east nor from the west, but from God.

In the family of God, the new converts (or recruits) as well as the young in Christ, are considered as newborn babes who, figuratively, are desirable of the sincere milk of the word, that they may grow thereby (1 Pet. 2 :2, 2 Cor. 3, Heb, 5:12-14).

The converts (recruits), therefore, should be trained to be aware, lest any spoil them through philosophy and vain deceit, after the tradition of men, after the rudiments of the world, and not after Christ' (Col. 2:8).

...

Therefore, in the same manner that the soldiers regurgitate their prayer hundreds of times until it shapes their identity, recruits in God's Kingdom are expected to pray without ceasing and model the word of God until it shapes their identity.

Like the soldiers with their prayers, the people of God are expected to be trained in the word of God. They must be trained to pray and to believe in the word of God until the word of God is reflected in them. Converts *must* reflect the attributes of the divine. Just like the soldiers who are trained to have the strongest bond of comradeship to those who belong to the order, Christian recruits *must* be trained to be their brother's keeper.

And, in the same manner that a prayer was instrumental in shaping the minds of the soldiers in training, the word of the Lord must be the main ingredient in the believer's battle. The word of the Lord must be taught in simplicity, rehearsed diligently, digested spiritually, applied with practicality, and lived daily in the uprising, down sitting, going out, and coming in of the believer and be inherited by future generations—or, a generation will come, that knows not the Lord (Judges 2:10).

The teaching and training in the word of the Lord is the only antidote to survive amidst the treacherous eventualities of breaches and open doors in systems and societies. It is the only weapon that can avert the wiles of the devil. The devil is defeated by the words of testimony and the blood of the Lamb. Therefore, let the word of the Lord dwell in you richly, teaching and admonishing one another in psalms and hymns and spiritual songs (Col. 3:16).

Chapter Four
Physical and Spiritual Connection

Sitting in mother's living room and watching my grandmother going up and down the stairs that led to the laundry room got me thinking. She came over for the Christmas holidays and chose to spend a few extra days with us—but she busied herself as though she was trying to earn her keep. Since the passing of grandpa, her visits had become more frequent. And even though she never intimated that she was lonely, I knew she needed the company. Sitting there looking at her nimbleness caused me to think of the extended family. Right there in the room were three generations of women. We were almost always apart from each other, yet there was this deep spiritual connection that made it feel as though we were always together.

Nevertheless, my mother and I didn't share the same opinion on most things. She was a bit of an over-thinker, and I was sometimes spontaneous. She would plan and even schedule her shopping trips. I simply shop when I needed something.

However, my mother and her siblings were all the same, cut from the same fabric and tightly woven together. But, believe it or not, they had bitter quarrels that brought them to the edge of fights at the dinner table. Quarrels in which venom spewed and subliminal characteristics that might have otherwise lay dormant, emerged. Those fights usually end with my mother yelling and pounding the table with her fist like a judge's gavel—silverware and chinaware bouncing up and down with each impact that accompanied her scream. And, when she captured the attention of everyone present, she would regurgitate one of grandma's overused biblical phrase—'*get it together and never let the sun go down on your wrath.*' At which time, the toxic energy in the room would dissipate and the tension deescalate at an alarming speed followed by seemingly sincere apologies and awkward moments of silence—at times, outbursts of laughter and tomfoolery.

One of my mother's sisters lived in Mandeville, Jamaica, and the other in London, England. They never needed an invitation to visit. And, their visits weren't limited to holidays. They'd drop in at times without warning like an inquisitive neighbor. Though they lived in other countries, they acted as if they were living a stone's throw away. Our home was like a haven for them—it was as if it was their oasis in a dry and thirsty world, or maybe there was just something special about Boston, Massachusetts.

Mom had told them of my dilemma while I was in the hospital, and they were on the next flight over. When they got here, they harassed me almost as much as my assailant. But I allowed them. They clung to me like leeches. They pulled down my bra straps and handled me as if they were preparing me for a mammogram. They even pried open my thighs to see the bruises—cursing and swearing at the sight of each abrasion. And, when I told them the story, they tried to implicate everyone present at the bar that night. Even the professor was amongst the suspects, because he gave the villain the fist-bump—they called the charges aiding and abetting. Moment by moment, they meticulously mulled over every aspect of the encounter and sought ways to police and convict the attacker themselves.

Their attitude caused me to think of the men in their lives, as well as my two uncles. My grandmother described the uncles as chips off the old block—stating that they were just like grandpa. In addition, she claimed that the in-laws and the uncles were birds of a feather.

I thought, however, that they were simple—conservative, and soft. Country bumkins, I might add, very different from their complex counterparts. They would go on catch and release fishing trips, fool themselves at golfing, and waste their time cat calling provocatively dressed women when they hang out together smoking Cuban cigars.

One of the uncles live in Florida with his family and the other in California with his family. And though they did not visit as often as my aunties—except in times of celebration and when they had problems with their wives, their less than frequent visits probably benefitted them, because they never seem to get justice from my mother when they complained about their wives. They were always in the wrong, even when it seemed as though they were right. Nevertheless, they never stopped complaining to mom.

My dad, however, was the outlier. He was somewhat absent. He had chosen another family—or however the story goes. Yet, his random letters, corny text messages, and oddly timed phone calls to mom and me kept him relevant. He was a Casanova of some sorts and that could be seen in his mannerism—he would call and sometimes mail me little tokens just because it was Monday, or Tuesday, or because it rained.

I sometimes wondered if he missed mom—or if his thoughtful contacts were jabs aimed at making her out to be the villain. Yet, if you'd asked her, you'd realize that she never cared to explain. Judge her if you please, but you would leave with no more information than you came with.

She never kept my dad and I apart either, yet she never made effort to be together. She cocooned herself in her world and closed the door to the past.

When I think of my family, I think of them as perfectly imperfect. I would not trade them for the world. The bittersweet relationship that they sometimes express was mindboggling, their quarrels and fights were distasteful and entertaining, and the unity among them was authentic, pure, and binding.

I am the vine, you are the branches. He who abides in me, and I in him, bears much fruit; for without me you can do nothing.

John 15:5

Jasmine had a chance to exhale, gather her thoughts, and reflect on her family. And, though she never told us of her aunties and uncles' professions, we can infer, based on their lifestyle, that they were not below the poverty margin—for the mere fact that they traveled whenever they pleased, golfed, and smoked Cuban cigars at leisure.

It is noteworthy to mention too, that though they lived in other countries, and different states, the family was not disjointed. Each set of family members were more of a subset that was connected to the whole. In that, when the crisis occurred, like phagocytes, they mobilized and came together.

More importantly, the siblings and the in-laws were connected by blood and the bond of marriage, respectively, and the relationship between all the parties involved was cemented through constant communication, mutual respect, and the power of love.

In similar regard, the armed forces are on point with the physical structure and its connection or interrelationship with the different entities of its whole. Whether or not they seem disjointed because of the location of the bases, or the name that they are given; the Army, Navy, and Air Force, are subsets of the armed forces of the country that governs them.

For the sake of efficiency and accountability, each of these entities are broken down into units, contingencies, squadrons, or battalions, in which each provides a different service. For example, the Support and Services Battalion provides food, clothing and equipment, weapons, and transportation for all the battalions.

The Infantry recruits, trains, and produces fighting men for their battalions, and men in the rest of the armed forces.

The Air Force contains a group of specialists who operate aircrafts; for example, passenger planes, helicopters, fighting jets, and bombers, to support the government and the needs of the other units.

The Coast Guard or Navy patrols the seas and keep the borders safe from foreign intervention, while the Engineering Division, consisting of soldiers professionally trained in structural and electrical engineers, build houses, roads, bridges, strong holds, and underground bunkers.

The contingents are further broken down into companies named after the phonetic alphabet for example: Alpha, Bravo, Delta, Echo, Charlie, and Headquarter. This is done to better manage and account for soldiers, and to operate efficiently.

Companies are broken down into platoons, sections, and squads. Soldiers are selected at company levels and trained in special courses to form units, which include Intelligence Unit (spy), who isolate themselves from the rest of the soldiers, and even when they are with their own, they cannot be easily identified.

Then, there is the Medical Unit, which includes the hospital and its staff of doctors, nurses, medics, and first aiders.

Other units include clerks, firemen, signals, demolition experts, drummers, and cooks.

However, every soldier is first trained as an infantry, and then posted to different units. And, though they are posted to other units, everyone works mechanically, in one accord, to achieve one purpose, which is the smooth running of the armed forces.

Note too, that the armed forces have every facility that is in the civil population. They have their own supermarket, gas station, church, cemetery, computer center, school, park, courthouse, and prison; you name it, they have it—all this is to show that the armed forces are connected to and interdependent on its own and can be independent of the civil society if the need should arise.

Nevertheless, the structural routines, facilities, and operations, are masterminded not only by the hierarchy of the armed forces, but also by the head of the government. In this, the very spirit and power of the government permeates the entire organization.

...

Although the armed forces contain a manmade structure, physically assembled by intelligence, there is a spiritual embodiment weaved into its system to promote the army's demeanor. Think about the presence of military men and women when there is turmoil—they strike fear into the very enemy, and reassurance and hope to captives. At times their very outlook commands the submission of the inferior warrior, even though the inferior warriors may be professionally trained.

This interwoven personification of intimidation, or of hope and liberation, are not only physically implanted, but also spiritually affixed, through the connection and authority of the powers of the government behind them that influence their disposition.

In the same sense that everything in nature produces after its kind, the soldiers' deportment physically expresses the mind of their hierarchy—they produce after their kind. In that, a weak government cannot give rise to a strong army. Instead, weak governments will produce weak and frustrated soldiers, or rebels—soldiers without purpose and drive.

If the soldiers are lacking in training, equipment, and optimum hierarchical structure and support, they are as fallible as a captive. Structure and connection therefore provide stability and reliability, give assurance, and enhance support.

...

The structure that is evident in Jasmine's family and that which is seen in the armed forces can also be seen in the church. Jasmine's family is connected through blood and the union of marriage.

The armed forces are connected through the interdependency of its subsets and alliances—and though they are not connected by blood, they pledge allegiance and are bonded by like-passion, and similar purpose.

...

The believers in the body of Christ are connected to each other by the spirit of God. Connection to the spirit of God is done through the adoption or marriage into the body of Christ. This opportunity was provided before the beginning of time—and in time, was ratified by the blood of Jesus Christ (Rom, 5:8, Rom. 8:29, 1Pet. 1:20, Eph. 1:4).

Since the connection to the spirit of God was provided by the redemptive process of Jesus, that means, it cannot be attained through works of righteousness. It was given through God's grace and must be received through faith. This is done so that every human being can have the same opportunity to freely accept or reject the salvation of God through the adoption into his family (Gal. 4 v 1:8, 1John 3v1-2).

In essence, that which qualifies a person to be a part of the Kingdom of God, or a part of the body of Christ, and to be connected to his spirit, is for that person to be born again. In which regard, the recipient goes through the process of being baptized in the name of Jesus Christ, for the remission of sins, and being filled with the gift of the Holy Spirit.

...

In this regard, unlike the armed forces that have permanent physical sites or locations, the body of Christ, or the Kingdom of God, does not. This is so because the Kingdom is represented through the believers.

The Kingdom is therefore manifested through the believer in the form of the seven gifts of the spirit and through the nine fruits of the spirit.

The quintessence of the matter is that the body of the believer becomes the temple of the living God in which the Holy Spirit dwells. The church, therefore, has nothing to do with a concrete structure. The concrete structure, or the physical site, is simply a meeting place for worship.

The church is the people.

And the people, is the body of Christ.

Therefore, the people form the battalions, the people form the units, the people form the contingents, the platoons, the companies, the sections, and the squads. The people, guided by the leaders of the five-fold ministry and the head of the body, Jesus Christ.

Here, the body of Christ is connected by the Spirit of God.

We notice that Jasmine's family took care of each other

especially in times of crisis. However, the believer in the body of Christ does not only think about his or her immediate family. Instead, the believers' thoughts, works, and prayers, are on behalf of the pocket of the vineyard in which he or she is assigned and beyond. Therefore, the believers' prayers focus on the community, the nation, and at times generations—and to a greater extent, the believers' prayers are focused on global issues.

In other words, if the believer does not stay connected, and pray, the earth will spiral into chaos—but if the believer stands his or her ground and pray, God will hear from heaven, forgive the sins, and heal the land (2 Chron 7:14).

The prayer of the believer moves God and set angels in motion to effect change. Prayer is what keeps the world from plunging into utter darkness.

Regardless of what society believes, God governs in the affairs of men.

Let me be quick to remind us that there was a time in the distant past when kings, governors, and all political leaders used to depend upon God for direction. There was a time when leaders encounter or envision crisis in their nation, they would call for the spiritually connected prophets and ask them to seek God's face so that they might know how to navigate through tumultuous situations—and they usually receive a word from the Lord.

Ask Pharoah, king of Egypt, and he will tell you of Joseph; ask king Uzziah and he will tell you of Isaiah the prophet. Ask the rulers of Nineveh, and they will tell you about the prophet Jonah; ask the world that was, and they will tell you about Noah.

There was a time when spiritually connected leaders and ordinary men and women would prostrate before God in fasting and prayers seeking his face so that they might know what to do and what not to do.

There was a time when the sick used to call for the elders of the church and did not depend solely on modern medicine that we enjoy today—the medicine that gives more side effects than it is able to cure (James 5:14-16).

The leaders of the ages knew that connection to the spirit of God by being a part of the family of God was of optimum importance. They knew that when the financial sectors face bankruptcy, God had a word of knowledge; they knew that when the doctors and scientists cannot find cures, Jesus gives the gift of healing; they knew that when the enemy comes in like a flood and the devil pounces like a roaring lion, the believer discerns their spirit and prophesy their doom in such a way that heaven endorses whatever is said or done by the believer (Matt: 18:18-20).

Therefore, in the network of families that build communities that form societies, the believer's battle is to bring awareness to the masses so that they might realize that chaos in the family, community, and society, is a direct disconnection with God.

The believer should realize that the quintessence of the need to connect with the spirit of God is to reconcile the world to God and only in doing so can the chaos be averted or managed. The believer in the church must therefore situate him or herself, under leadership, stand his or her ground in purposeful ministry according to appointment and deployment, so that the glory of God might cover the earth as the waters the seas—knowing that the battle is the Lord's (1 Sam17:47).

Chapter Five
The Armor

An induced nostalgic state, brought on by the need to escape the stressful demands of study was what caused me to encounter the Ugly Drunk the first time. The toxic substance that my assailant poured into my drink, as well as prior need to escape the monotonous drag of family traditions, caused me to glimpse him the second time. This time, my curiosity was driving me to see him again on purpose.

Why not?

The reason I give is that he was the one who saved me from that horrible creature and a lifetime of shame—but truth be told, I found the Drunk fascinating the very first time I saw him. Maybe it was the unexpected charisma, the unconventional behavior, the conflict of societal expectations, the need for lawless animalistic pleasure, or maybe it was just the thrill of defying my mother's expectations and to prove that her moralistic gibberish was outdated and bizarre. Whatever it was, I just had this intense desire to see him again.

In my pursuit, I went to the precinct, introduced myself, updated the police officer at the help desk about the incident, and asked for the name of the gentleman who saved me from the monstrous villain and later gave a statement of the crime. But to my disappointment, the police officer stated that it was an ongoing investigation; therefore, it was against the protocols of the police department to give out any information about witnesses. It seemed a bit unusual to me, since I was the victim of the case in question.

I ended up leaving the police department without the information I sought.

It took me about four visits to Jamaica train station in Queens, and half a dozen visits to a basketball court in the vicinity where the crime took place before I counted my losses and gave up my search.

About two months or so later, I took the Amtrak train from Penn Station, New York, to Trenton, New Jersey, to meet with my mother and a few friends at a function. The coach in which I sat had a group of middle-aged white women who smiled courteously at every eye contact. Not wanting to be engaged into a conversation, I slipped away to the far end of the coach—away from the ladies. The low murmur of voices and sporadic laughter added to the serene ambience on the train. During the ride, I felt like using the restroom and so I went to the back of the adjoining coach to do so. Lo and behold, I heard the raised tone of the lecturing voice of an orator, speaking.

The pattern of his speech struck a chord in my memory. The speaker humored his chuckling audience, then his stern raspy voice brought them back to attention. It was as if he were a funny professor who mixed humor with enlightenment in his class.

The lecturer's use of rhetorical speech was attention grabbing and motivating. The voice caught my attention and held my interest. The same captivating repetitious punchlines that I heard months before were once more achieving the aim of keeping the listening audience, listening. His earnest appeal-of-a-call to invest was inspiring and thought provoking. And, his perky attitude and mannerism were infectious and inviting. It was the familiarity in his voice that had caused me to fearfully and hopefully turn and look. And to my surprise, it was the Ugly Drunk.

In that moment, my joy was full.

Nevertheless, in that same instance, upon examining the audience superficially, I noticed that the same elderly Caucasian man, smartly attired in suit and tie, unequivocally the Drunk's opposite, was there, asking questions and recording on his notepad—

Instantaneously, every alarm of suspicion in my cranium went off and it felt as though I was on the verge of blowing a fuse. I could not believe my eyes.

As a result of seeing the elderly Caucasian man with the Drunk on the train, I began to scrutinize the audience further. It was sprinkled with curious familiar faces from that train ride in Jamaica, Queens, months before—they were asking important questions and getting the encouragement and the knowledge they needed to invest. I swallowed hard, and almost choked on my own saliva. The Q&A covered all bases. It was an iron-clad scam. The players were the same, and though worded differently, the questions were the same. Only the audience was different. I realized then that the questions were fixed like those in a textbook; the answers were designed to elicit specific responses, and the intent was targeted and purposeful.

My need for the restroom dissipated as I ducked into a nearby seat and listened. I could not believe that I was witnessing a live scam in process. I wondered at what point I should let myself be seen, and if I would be recognized.

Then came the closing arguments and the referrals—the people were eating out of the palm of the Ugly Drunk. He then began to drop names of personal advisors who could help the audience create and maintain holistic financial plans—help them to build tax efficient portfolio, give 401k advice and approach to diversification, as well as insights on cashflow, spending, and budgeting. He was deep into the purses of the audience—pointing them to money management experts who guaranteed high returns and little to no risk.

I marveled at the efficiency in which he did his closing, his Q&A, and his referral. It was so set, that it neatly fitted into the time the train took to reach Trenton and pulled into the station.

I got up and continued to the restroom, but I couldn't use it. I went back to the coach and walked towards him as the train slowed into the station. It was his stop as well. I smiled and nodded at him, holding his gaze. He courteously smiled back and turned his eyes away and then quickly back at me. "I know you" he said, pointing his index finger with childlike enthusiasm, "how have you been?"

"I'm doing great, so glad to see you again, how are you?" I asked, with nervous excitement and skepticism. His demeanor softens, as he gingerly proposed questions that checked my comfort level on the subject and when he realized that I was not reluctant in speaking, he began to speak of how terrible he felt the night when he delivered me from my assailant.

We stepped off the train and spoke for a while. And, without my asking, he mentioned that the license plate of the would-be rapist was from a junk yard and was previously registered to a deceased person, and that except the pictures the camera captured in the bar, and those at a stoplight that he ran, the police did not have enough information to track him; therefore, the investigation was ongoing.

I got more information from the Ugly Drunk than the police officer was willing to share.

Within five minutes, one conversation led to the next, and I pointedly asked him of the purpose of his crusade.

"How does it work?" I asked.

"How does what work?" he answered seemingly lost.

I pointed towards the train and the people, "Jamaica, Queens, now Trenton, New Jersey, and who knows where else. How does it work?"

"You mean the discussion with my friends?" he smiled and gave me a mouthful of philosophical garbage about the need to invest, but when he was done answering, I asked him the question again.

"How does it work? A mean, apparently, it's a business—that can be seen in your passion, so how does it work?" he went off on another tangent trying to sound like Mother Theresa.

I held his gaze, explained to him that I was still in school but had a little stash that my grandmother secured for me, and I would like some advice from his people on how to invest it. That was when, for the first time, I heard him stammer. I smiled at him. He smiled back. Right then, I held his gaze, expressionlessly. He chuckled and broke into laughter before he could fully finish asking how big a stash I was referring to.

I pursed my lips, shook my head in disappointment, held up my hands in resignation, and started to walk away without heeding to his woeful appeal. As I walked away, I could not help but to think of the many people who fell for the scam and would have their Nest Eggs swindled by the footmen of a Ponzi scheme who posed like knights in shining armor.

Jasmine came to realize that her hero was the point man of an elaborate scam. A scam that she considered to be iron-clad and impenetrable. In that, though the end game was money, the Ugly Drunk never asked his audience for any; instead, he suggested a path to financial stability, offered security, made referrals, and vouched for the integrity of the experts he recommended.

It was impenetrable because those in collusion were strategically positioned and preprepared with questions designed to elicit answers that were tied into trust, loyalty, and transparency—ideas that audiences gravitated towards. And, having as icing, an elderly in collusion to authenticate its pseudo legitimacy.

The Drunk's scheme was impenetrable because he and his cohorts covered every ground, left no room for doubt, and left nothing to chance. He knowledgeably and efficiently answered the why, the when, and the how, with ease and relaxation.

He was not only charismatic in charming the middle-aged housewives into second-guessing investing their nest eggs, but he also had a structure, he was business oriented and executed excellent time management skills. His modeling session in which he advertised his product as well as his Q&A were succinct and tailored, so much so, that his content and delivery could only be otherwise captured in an abbreviated version of an insurance coverage plan.

And, to showcase his professionalism, his presentation neatly fitted into the train's schedule, so that he was done in time before the train slowed into the station.

...

Jasmine stressed that the scammers presentation was iron-clad and impenetrable. They acted as though they were aware that service providers must first be trustworthy, and so they sold themselves as such. They armored themselves under an umbrella of service knowledge and preyed on the vulnerability of the unassuming passengers that they addressed.

In the same manner that the scammers covered themselves under a psychological armor so that they might appear authentic, soldiers clad themselves with physical armors for bodily protection against the enemy and other eventualities.

Nevertheless, the specifics of the physical armor of soldiers have changed over the years; these changes are due to the changing methods of war. Uniform outfit is the simplest but is a unique armor that covers the soldier. It includes the helmet, camouflage jackets and slacks, boots, and guns.

The color, type, and style of the uniform may vary based on the ground that the soldiers occupy. These variations are geared to create a blend or camouflage with the immediate surrounding. The helmet, made of fiberglass or steel, is a protective gear for the head, constructed in an oval shape to deflect, at an angle, any object that has direct contact with it. Further to that, it has a mesh on the inside attached to the sides below the roof in which the head fits neatly into; this apparatus acts as a shock absorber in the event that the helmet suffers a blunt blow.

His jacket and trousers made of course linen, protects the soldier from harsh weather condition and rough terrain. The linen jacket and slacks also provide floatation when inflated in water.

His girded waistband has a yoke attached over his shoulders at the front and anchored in the waistband at the rear. Pouches are attached to the waistband to carry ammunitions, water, and medication. This waistband is so set to hinge ropes to anchor apparatus of parachute and ropes for rappelling so the soldier can maneuver air drops and mountainous terrain.

He also has a large pack on his back, which contains his personal effects, bedding and meals ready to eat.

He wears tall upper boots that are water and oil resistant. The bottom of the boot though flexible, has rigid contours and a smooth hollow at the instep, this is fitted for obstacle course and rope climbing. The innersole contains a thin sheet of metal to protect the feet from protruding instruments, which can be harmful to the feet.

In addition, the soldier carries a rifle as his personal weapon, which is fixed with a bayonet for close quarter combat; in addition to that, he sometimes carries a side arm.

In volatile situations there are added equipment to aid him in further protection; for example, bulletproof vest, shields, and armored tanks; these however are not a part of his daily wear, but a compliment when necessary.

Additionally, as hinted in chapter three, the most potent armor of the soldier lies within the power of his trained mind. A trained mind possesses the capability to be proactive, quick-thinking, and decisive under stress and in dangerous situations. This mindset will enable the soldier to take measures that will prevent future repercussions and thereby protect himself and his hierarchy.

We can conclude then that the soldier's armor is so designed to assist him in maneuvers to physically protect his body and the orders of his superior.

...

In the believers' battle, the believers are engaged in a spiritual conflict with the devil and his cohorts and are told, 'be strong in the Lord and in the power of his might.' The believers are instructed by the Lord to put on the whole armor of God that they may be able to stand against the wiles of the devil.

Therefore, unlike the scammers, whose mental fortitude or verbal craft covered them on a psychological and social platform, and the soldiers whose armor covers them physically, the believers armor covers them spiritually and extends to their natural and psychological endeavors. This is so because the believers do not wrestle with flesh and blood; instead, they wrestle with principalities and powers, against the rulers of the darkness of this world, and against spiritual wickedness in high places. In other words, the believers wrestle with opponents in the spiritual realm as well as the spirits that control the diabolical hierarchy in the natural realm.

Therefore, the believers are instructed by God, to stand, having on the helmet of salvation, the breastplate of righteousness; having their loins girt about with truth and feet shod with the preparation of the gospel of peace, taking the shield of faith, wherewith he or she shall be able to quench the fiery darts of the wicked, and the sword of the spirit which is the word of God: praying always with all prayer and supplication in the spirit, and watching thereunto with all perseverance and supplication for all saints (Eph. 6: 11-18).

Here, the believers' combatant attire is likened unto the attire of the Roman soldiers of the olden days—as present-day soldiers do not have metal breastplates, swords, and shields. Thus, the language is used figuratively to indicate complete provision of spiritual virtues necessary to fight against evil.

The helmet of salvation therefore refers to the spirit of the mind, which when trained in the word of God, is so designed to discern every spirit and take authority over every thought and high thing that exalts itself against the knowledge of God.

The trained mind defies worldly logics. It is not concerned with the problems; instead, it sees the solution. In other words, it is a battle of faith. In that, the believer must believe only in the report of the Lord regardless of circumstances.

It is a mindset and belief that is endowed with the authority and the ability to speak as God spoke and to call the things that are not, as though they are—hence, speaking things into being.

The scripture states that it is not by strength nor might but by my spirit says the Lord.

Therefore, the weapons of our warfare are not carnal but mighty through Christ to the pulling down of strong holds.

Nevertheless, even though the battle is the Lord's, the believers must be on an all-time ready and be fully aware, so that they are not overtaken by temptation. In that regard, the helmet of salvation is a part of the spiritual adornment and warfare equipment that should be a part the believers' daily attire.

The breastplate of righteousness is practical righteousness in daily life to protect the heart; the heart in this context would be one's personality, conscience, and will to live holy (Isa. 59:17).

Loins girded with truth is all about personal honesty, sincerity, dependability and trust—God desires truth in the inward parts (Ps. 51:6).

The feet shod with the gospel deals with preparedness of skillful knowledge to pronounce the gospel with soundness irrespective of circumstances (Isa. 52:7).

The sword of the spirit, which is the word of God, is the believer's offensive weapon to convict, correct, heal, redeem, drive out demons and to overcome all evil.

Under the countless blessings of salvation, the armor of God is one of the most crucial possessions in the believer's battle. In that, it incorporates an extension of protection under Christ' blood. Saying that to say, a person can be living in a Jet stream of blessing but is not covered under the blood of Jesus Christ.

The mere fact that God falls the rain on the just and on the unjust is evidence that blessings do not mean covering. Everyone is blessed in one way or the other, but not everyone is covered. When a person is under the covering of the almighty, it means that that person's life is blessed regardless of economic status (Ps. 32:1).

The covering, or the armor in this case, does not only cover the individual who has attained grace, it is extended to his or her family. God cares about the family of his loved ones and answers prayers concerning them. An example in the Old Testament is that it was a common practice for Job to repent and offer prayers and sacrifices to God on behalf of his children (Job. 1:5).

In the New Testament, Martha's testimony was that 'if Jesus was there, her brother would not have died (Jn. 11:21). It is evident then that Jesus cares about the loved ones of his people.

Jasmine probably believed that she was lucky when she escaped the rapist's plan—that could not have been farther from the truth. Luck does not deliver a person in warfare—prayers do.

She probably thought it was because of her astuteness or meticulous observation of the scammers why she caught onto them on the train to New Jersey, but truth be told, it might have been her mother's prayers, or prayers that she herself had prayed in the past that caused her to get the revelation, or it might be a believer on duty in her neighborhood who was standing in the gap and was praying for the protection of the people in the community.

An example of someone standing in the gap that was modeled in scriptures is the story of Abraham and his nephew, Lot.

God had promised Abraham the blessing, and because of Abraham's blessing, his nephew Lot, over in Sodom, was covered. God would not destroy Sodom, with Lot, without telling Abraham first (Gen. 18:17).

Here, Abraham was given the privilege or opportunity to negotiate the terms so that they might benefit his nephew, Lot.

Like Abraham, the believer, when under the armor of God, is able to effect change in the lives of the immediate family, then his or her duties extend to the society in which he or she belongs, or in the pocket of the vineyard where God placed him or her.

As a result, God now exposes the welfare and state of living of the neighbors, friends, associates, and society to the believer so that the believer can pray for God to heal their land. Hopefully, they will accept salvation in the end because it is the goodness of God that leads men to salvation (Rom. 2:4).

In other words, whatever there is to befall individuals under the covering, is seen by the believer in advance. For the secret of the Lord is with them that fear him—for further illustration you could see the full story of Abraham and his nephew Lot, and the bargain Abraham had with God over the welfare of Lot.

Another example of God protecting the loved ones of the people who serve him is in the case of Noah. The scripture says that Noah also was forewarned of the flood to come and moved with fear to protect his household (Heb. 11:7).

These insights, inspirations and vision that accompany the armor of God are not for mere knowledge. It is to protect the domain and inhabitant of the assigned. Hence the armor of God does not only convey spiritual protection, but the physical well-being is also protected.

...

When I was growing up, I used to spend a lot of time reading. And, when I exhausted my favorite reading materials, out of boredom, I turned to textbooks, the dictionary, and eventually the Bible. I found then that I began to develop a passion for the stories of the Old Testament—David and Goliath, Samson and the Philistines, Esau and Jacob, Ruth and Naomi, Abraham and Lot, Nebuchadnezzar king of Babylon, to name a few. Those stories were so intriguing, they kept me turning the pages, so much so, that I read chapters at a time.

It was not as though my parents were devoutly religious; we attended an Anglican church on Sundays and observed Christian values, but we were not ardent Christians. Nevertheless, I found myself craving for these stories, falling in love with the protagonist of each story, and before I knew it, I was even skimming through the pages of the New Testament.

I never cared about the spiritual implications or meaning of the scriptures that I read, I was simply being entertained by the characters.

Simultaneously, with my newfound love of the Bible stories, I started to have dreams. Weird dreams. Dreams that sometimes were happening while I was dreaming. I tried not to place emphasis on the correlation between the dreams and my love of Bible stories, but the two commenced at the same time and seem to impact each other.

I used to tell these dreams to my best friend and the two of us used to watch as the dreams come to pass as if we were watching live shows.

As I recalled, I had this dream in which I saw my grandfather vomiting. And I being inquisitive, went closer and stood over him, looking. I could distinguish specks of red mucous in his vomit. In the same instance, a voice in my head said that he was vomiting out his liver.

As soon as I awoke that morning and left my room, I saw my grandfather in the same position as I saw him in the dream, vomiting. I nervously went and stood over him to investigate. Lo and behold, I saw the same picture that I saw in the dream. The entire pool of vomit was freckled with red specks of mucous.

My grandfather went to the doctor later that day, and I went and told the dream to my friend.

When my grandfather returned from the doctor's office, I was quite eager to hear of his diagnosis, and so I listened for the news. The doctor, he said, told him that he drank too much alcohol, it was destroying his liver.

Pages would not allow if I should tell of all the nightly dreams and their actual occurrences. At that time, however, I was immature and sportily watched as the good dreams came to pass, and fearfully watched as the bad ones take their course—not understanding the gifts and callings, not understanding what it meant to be covered under the blood of Jesus, not knowing what it meant to be the watchman over a family, not understanding that I had a say in what happened and what did not; not understanding that people perish, because of lack of knowledge (Hos. 4:6).

I still did not grasp the real intent of the dreams until early one morning I had a dream in which my grandfather called and gave me instructions to lead his donkey to one of his farms.

In that vision, I was walking through a lonely gorge with the donkey. While I walked, I threw stones at grass quits and mongoose alike, as I went through the narrow ravine. When I got to a certain spot in the ravine, I bent down to pick up fresh stones and something terrifying happened that my memory never got a chance to registered before I was awakened out of my sleep, at the sound of my grandfather voice—calling me to wake up and to carry the donkey to the farm.

I was a nervous wreck when I heard my grandfather's instructions, knowing that I just had the dream and not knowing the frightening end result. Therefore, I calculated in my mind to take an alternate route other than the one I saw in the dream, which was the river route—only to hear my grandfather yelling a threatening like warning that I should not take the river route, because the river had overflowed its banks resulting from the previous rains.

With that, I went to one of my friends who had early morning duties on a farm close to ours. I tried fervently to persuade him, and others who came by, to accompany me—without telling them the dream, but as if planned, or forewarned, they all unusually declined with silly excuses of impending errands.

The journey was for me alone and I cautiously and fearfully took it. Upon entering the narrow ravine, I remembered that I was throwing stones at the grass quits and mongoose, but nature was at its best that morning and the birds came out in abundance.

The temptation was too much for me not to heed and so I started picking up and throwing stones—and so set the dream in motion.

As I neared the blank spot of the dream, I cautiously approached, slowing my pace and inching along the narrow ravine, trembling. The birds however were just too much for me not to have sport, so I bent down to pick up another hand full of pebbles. Right there at the blind spot of the dream, right there where my memory did not register the event, right there at that pivotal point where the fears brewed, a terrible shriek of anguish gash through my lungs and pain shot up my body.

I think I might have broken Usain Bolt's record that morning; because, since I screamed, I was a hundred meters away—the donkey had bitten me on my butt! I ran so fast and screamed so hard but was relieved later to know that the ordeal was finally over.

...

Since the day the donkey bit me on the butt, I began to pray and ask God not to make the bad dreams come to pass. Yes, I was selfish enough to learn from my own bad experience.

However, I began to look forward for dreams and surely, they came, some of the revelations tarried, some instantaneously came to pass. Years later I found that I was in training or better yet, I was being prepared.

I got saved. The warfare began. The dreams continued. My knowledge increased, I learned to be wise as a serpent and harmless as a dove, slow to speak and quick to hear, standing still and seeing the salvation of the Lord.

It is a good feeling to know that the secret of the Lord is with them that fear him. It's beautiful to understand the deep things of the Lord. It is such a joy when you can hear from the Lord and help someone overcome his or her trials. It is even more satisfying, when you are asked, and is able to give directions that establish purpose. Yet, it is scary to see them that you hold in high esteem doing forbidden deeds and ministering on flower-decked podiums. Frightening, it is, when you have a dream of someone and hear the stories later of the actual occurrences. It leaves guilt and fear and the lingering thoughts and questions such as: should I have told the person what I dreamt? Did I receive a message to tell? Why did I not pray hard enough and ask God to change the course?

...

The point here is that the believer becomes the guardian of family, friends, and the neighborhood or the pocket of the vineyard that the Lord put him or her over when he or she has on the armor of God.

The anointing is extended. The package contains loved ones, they are a part of the menu, they are in the dish, don't let them die; stop the leprosy from affecting them even before the symptoms appears, deliver them from that which is cancerous and whatsoever is said to be terminal—pray, so that God can heal the land.

Where there are traditions and hereditary curses, God's hands are not short, he is not a man that he can lie, he is not slack as men count slackness, he is able to do exceedingly, abundantly, above that which we can ask or think. And, he did promise that anything we ask, believing, it shall be done unto us (Mark 11:24).

Remember too, that he came to heal the broken heart and to set at liberty them that are bruised, this is the reason he received those stripes.

...

I had a beloved friend, passionately called Vel, an evangelist, we had become friends through trade and travel. One night in a dream, I saw the spirit of death barreling to and fro through the earth, guided by what seemed like a train track path. The spirit tore through buildings and over landscapes laying tracks as it went by, leaving behind screams of pain and horror and a black fog of smoke. In the same dream, I saw my friend Vel in a restaurant, perspiring profusely, because of the tremendous heat in the building. In the same instance, I heard an explosion and saw her head literally exploded as the spirit of death barreled through her building leaving behind tracks liken unto that on which trains travel.

When I woke up, I began speaking in the heavenly and pulling down strongholds, binding the spirit and rendering it powerless, null and void, speaking against everything that exalted itself against God and his people.

Later that day, I went to see Vel in the arcade where she operates her business. She greeted me excitedly and before I could return the compliments, she anxiously started to give me details of her tragic death, that a friend of hers dreamt.

Though it felt a bit insensitive to be the bearer of similar bad news, I told Vel what I too, had dreamt. And, in the same breath, encouraged her that we shouldn't spend time worrying; instead, we should pray.

Interestingly, a few months later, Vel started a restaurant business. The business was doing well, but she complained that the heat in the kitchen was unbearable. She said the vents were blocked and the heat from the fire was trapped and circulated instead of going out, thus affecting everyone in the kitchen.

One Saturday I went to have lunch at her place. When I saw her, her visage was the spitting image of what I had seen in the dream—and to make matters worse, she was sweating profusely.

Incidentally, when I took a second look, I realized that I was standing in the exact place where I was standing in the dream. The same spot where I heard the explosion of her head—right then, without her knowing, I began praying and rebuking the spirit of death.

God had it that the rent was too expensive; therefore, when the landlord refused to renegotiate or fix the dysfunctional facilities, she had to make the decision to relocate and thus was saved. Her protection came because of the covering of the armor of God—in this regard, we can say that to be forewarned is to be forearmed.

...

I told the story of Vel to my friend, Cy. It never struck him as a big deal. As far as he was concerned, the story never grabbed his attention. He didn't think that Vel would have died if she never closed the restaurant. He believed that there were too many probabilities and variables—as he called it—for him to believe that the prayer was why she moved and was saved.

Nevertheless, he confessed to me a few weeks later that he was watching television when he saw a shadow flashed by him. Instantaneously, the thought came to him that it was the spirit of death. Being a sceptic, he was a bit taken aback and so he questioned the reality of what he saw and settled for the conclusion that it was either a glare from the television, or he was hallucinating. He said he dosed off for a moment and his sister appeared before him in a dream-like trance, and he saw the shadow again, going by her. He told me later that he remembered the testimonies of mine, that God will tell his people things before they happen, so that that they can have a chance to stand in the gap peradventure he will have mercy.

Nevertheless, he shook off the thought, refreshed himself, and continued to watch the television.

A few hours later his phone rang, in reality, and he received the unfortunate news that his sister had passed away, suddenly—he blamed himself for years.

...

A few months later, his mother got very ill and was admitted in the University Hospital of the West Indies, the doctors had amputated one of her legs; nevertheless, the complications grew worse. The doctors finally gave her a month to live. Since her sickness was terminal, the family was in turmoil.

One evening Cy's wife lay down to take a rest from work, she saw in a vision, the form of an angel, flying in a pale form towards the hospital. Her spirit told her that it was an angel of death and so she began to rage war in her dream, fighting that spirit. When she awoke, the fighting continued through prayers, and she was victorious.

More than six months later, her mother-in-law was still alive—to the doctors' surprise. It was when her mother-in-law called and told the praying daughter-in-law that she was tired and wanted to go, that she slacked in her prayers in that area, that the mother-in-law finally passed away, peacefully.

...

Nevertheless, before I give the final testimony let me hurry to inform you that as a believer, when you are under the armor, praying fervently, living righteously, begin to hear the voice of God, have vision or dreams, and start seeing in the spirit—the devils will multiply themselves against you. The host of hell will break loose and launch attacks against you for you to leave them alone. More importantly, they will try to cross your lines—they will create noise, so that the voice of the Lord becomes indistinguishable in order for them to implant falsehood.

Nevertheless, some time ago, a friend of mine invited me to a church in New York, I accepted the invitation. The night before I went to the church, I had this bizarre dream in which I saw the pastor of the church beckoning to the ushers to bring out the bouquets of flowers that he had made—decking the altar and the podium to sell them to his congregants.

In the dream I found myself having a conversation with the pastor, a conversation in which I told him that he shouldn't actually make the altar the place where he sold his wares; instead, he should use the lobby, or a designated area, since the altar is a Holy place where the people come to Christ, and the podium is where the ministry of the choir and sacred activities take place.

Though I said those things in the dream, I knew that in reality I would never have opened my mouth. Nevertheless, right there in the church, in the dream, a pair of serpent eyes appeared behind the pastor and glared at me, each eye was as big as a man's head. I gasped and withdrew behind a column. Frightened, I awoke out of the dream, only to see the serpent eyes in my room hovering over me.

I rebuked so hard until I almost lost my voice, but it steadily glared at me unperturbed, came closer, then elevated itself to the roof and disappeared. My bed was soaked in perspiration. All of this happened the Saturday night.

The Sunday morning, I went to the church. After the offering—believe it or not—the pastor took the microphone and called for his ushers to come forward with the flowers. The ushers made trips upon trips and decked the altar and the podium with floral arrangements that the pastor had made. In my mind, all I was repeating was—oh, my, God.

To my surprise, the pastor, who had not known me prior, called me up, out of the audience, to pray. To be forewarned, is to be forearmed.

In essence, I am saying that the armor of God surrounds your entire endeavor and the people placed in your hands by God. In addition, there is a presence of angels in a fence-like hedge encamping around the believer and a halo-like perimeter, which no evil can break. The Christian's attire is then spiritual, giving health to personality, behavior, and attitude, protecting spirit, soul, and the body.

Chapter Six
Order of Battle

It has been seven months since the invitation to the New Year's Eve party, and nothing seems to be moving where my case was concerned. One afternoon my aunt and I were in New York City, shopping. I happened to look at my cell phone and noticed a missed call and a voicemail from the police precinct. Showing the screen to my overly dramatic auntie, she grabbed the phone, put it on speaker, listened the voice message and returned the call. After a minute of introduction and explanation, the receptionist, or the person who answered the phone, asked me to come to the station the next day at a specific time and ask for a certain policeman.

"Can we come today?" asked my auntie, impatiently, and with an attitude—not knowing what the meeting would be about.

"No ma'am, there are certain preparations to be made first," came the sober reply.

"And what preparations might those be?" she asks.

"I am sorry, but that cannot be disclosed at this time, ma'am," came the polite response.

"Auntie, can I have the phone, please?" I said, taking the phone from her and taking it off speaker. "I will be there, thank you so much for the information," I said to the person on the other end of the line and hung up.

My aunt was doing her last-minute shopping before she returned to Jamaica the next day. Would you believe it? She called the airline and canceled her flight immediately.

The next day we got to the precinct early. But it was as if they were waiting for us. One of the police officers who had come to the hospital and taken the report, along with a few other officers and men in suits, approached and greeted me. I introduced my aunt, and they asked her to wait on the outside. Then they asked me to accompany them into a little room. Asked me how I was doing and told me that they wanted me to identify a possibly suspect.

I immediately objected. I was a bit taken aback by the insane, unexpected, and abrupt request, until they explained that they believed it was connected to my case.

Would you believe it? Standing there in line, in-between two husky tattooed fellows, was my assailant. "Oh my God!" I gasped, hands covering my face! "Can they see me from behind this glass?" I asked in stammering surprise, already knowing the answer, not knowing what to say in the moment.

"Calm down, take it easy. Nobody can see you from here, but you must tell us if you see the person who harassed you on Christmas Eve of last year. Then you have to tell us which person it is."

"Christmas Eve!" I retorted with a frown.

"I'm sorry, um, New Year's Eve," he said, flipping through the pages on his clipboard.

I pointed at my assailant and called the number that he held, and the officer checked a few times to be sure that I was certain. Then told me afterwards that the case was going to be called up soon, and that I didn't have to be present at the preliminary hearing if I didn't want to be, but I will be notified when it is time for the actual trial.

The conversation felt a bit erratic, and rushed, and the police officer was staring me down while he spoke as though he was telling me not to report to court.

I left the room, joined my aunt, and explained what happened inside there to her. She was furious and as a result she verbally attacked the policeman with carefully selected words that bordered on disrespect.

"What do you mean by she doesn't have to report to court?" she asked, seeking clarity for the mumbo-jumbo that I repeated, "the last time she was here, some retard told her that the culprit could not be found, so now that the bastard is found, does that mean he will remain in custody until trial?"

"I am not sure, Ma'am, he might not remain in custody; that's left up to the judge's discretion. Already his lawyer is arranging bail for him. And to answer your first question, the preliminary hearing is what Jasmine does not have to attend, the real trail date will be announced, and she will be notified when to come to court."

"What do you mean might not remain in custody, why is he going on bail?"

"That is how the court system works, Ma'am you just have to trust the process the same way that everybody else is doing."

"Everybody else!" yelled my auntie, "are you speaking in general or are you saying that this dirtbag is a serial rapist?"

"Everything is speculative at this time. Your case might not be an isolated one. Nevertheless, I cannot give you any more information at this time. Already I have said too much, so go home now and we will be in touch."

Three weeks later the policeman who had been staring me down called. Stating that the trial would be the next day and he had forgotten to inform me. I could not believe it. *'What a convenient memory loss'* I thought to myself. Deep down, I felt it was deliberate, but I had no proof. I told my mother. She sprang from around her computer and went to her closet.

"Mom, you don't—"

"I know. We'll be fine."

I dialed my auntie in Jamaica. At first mention of the date, she hung up the phone. I redialed her number a few times, but her phone rang without an answer. All this time my mom kept smiling.

"What?" I asked, confused.

"She's trying."

"Who is trying? And trying what?"

"Your auntie."

Half an hour later the phone rang, it was auntie, and she was cursing like a fisherman, telling me how she was trying to get on a flight, but that all the flights were filled for the next day, and that she would be on standby. "Auntie, you were just here the other day, you don't have to inconvenience yourself. I was just keeping you abreast when I called."

"That's fine. That's fine. I am abreast."

The next day my mother and I got to the courthouse early and sat at the back of the courtroom. When the case was called up and the clerk mentioned my name, and the names of a few other ladies' the room went silent. The defendant's lawyer looked at me and then he scanned the room with wide-eye-jaw-dropping-shock, as though he didn't expect to see me or the other ladies sitting there.

He then asked the judge for a sidebar. When granted, I read his lips and realized that he was asking the judge for a continuance. Nevertheless, I couldn't determine the rest of his conversation by reading his lips, probably because of the inaudible courthouse language that I didn't quite understand. However, his body language appeared like that of a guilty child in front of a principal. I could thereby tell that he was making an apologize to the judge for an inconvenience, or he was making a farfetched request. The judge seemed infuriated. Probably not willing to accept an apology or concede to whatever erroneous request he might have had. She flipped through the file and asked aloud for the police who took my initial evidence. The police told the judge that the statement that he originally took was misplaced.

Again, the judge addressed the lawyers in their courthouse verbiage, and I knew enough to know that she was verbally chastising everyone involved with the handling of the case. She made an announcement, gave them twenty-four hours, then banged her gavel.

I waited a few moments and then left the courtroom, disoriented, uncertain of what truly went on. My mother went straight to the policeman, looked him up and down, then said, "How could you?" and walked away. I motioned to her and turned the opposite direction, looking for the lady's room.

Missing my turn, I came up on a room in which I heard the defendant's lawyer's voice.

"What are they doing here," he asked. "I thought you said they wouldn't appear. I expected the case to be thrown out."

"That's true," said the other, "they never came to any of the initial hearings, and they weren't supposed to be here today either. I am not sure what happened."

I hurried back to my mother after I heard what the men said, held her arm, and literally dragged her from the courthouse.

"They are all working together, Mom. The culprits are all working together."

"You mean those crooked cops?"

"Yes, mother. As if it wasn't clear enough in the courtroom, I heard the lawyer in a room telling someone that we weren't supposed to show up today."

"Don't mind them, my child. The scales of justice are balanced. Everyday bucket goes to the well, one day the bottom will fall out. Justice will be served, in this life, or the next."

The eyes of the Lord are in every place, beholding the evil and the good.

Proverbs 15:3

Jasmine has been caught up into a warfare that was beyond the scope of her imagination. The chaos that surrounded her was like a mild whirlwind brewing into a tsunami.

The process that preceded her destination is what soldiers call the "order of battle" or "battle preparation drills" as mentioned before. In this process—like the soldiers preparing for their impending war—the devil sets the stage for future devastation.

In setting the stage, several irregularities must happen to disrupt the natural flow or the foundation where an individual stands—sometimes the things that happen are trivial, simple inconveniences that are not worth attending to.

These inconveniences are brought on by human desires: the lust of the flesh, the lust of the eyes, and the pride of life. Therefore, battle preparation mostly deals with what the senses perceive, how the senses register what has been perceived, and how the spirit of the person reacts to the stimuli.

In addition, a person becomes a captive only when that person is drawn away by his or her own lust and is enticed. The scripture states that, every man is tempted, when he is drawn away of his own lust, and enticed. Then when lust hath conceived, it bringeth forth sin: and sin, when it is finished, bringeth forth death (James1:13-15). Therefore, it's the enemies' job to create the scenarios that will cause a person to naturally be enticed.

In Jasmine's case, several inconveniences had been set into motion over the period and the results evolved as though they had haphazardly happened. The latest fruits of her works are as follows: one, the Drunk, who was supposed to be her key witness, was a scammer—that means, he does not have much credibility in a court of law. Two, she did not officially receive a date to attend court. Three, the police gave her the information just a few hours before her case was scheduled to begin—this was the same police, whom it appeared as if was indirectly telling her not to show up to court. Four, based on the conversation she overheard in the room with the defendant's lawyer, they were in collusion with the police. Five, the police somehow misplaced her original statement. And six, as simple as it might seem, her inquisitive auntie couldn't get on a plane to observe, ask pertinent questions, or to give her moral support.

Note that the knowledge of these irregularities sent Jasmine's mind into a tailspin. And, instead of taking a step back to observe and analyze the situation, she acted on impulse, grabbed her mother by the arm and darted from the courthouse. It can be inferred by her actions that she believed that the members of the justice system were tilting the balance of the scales towards the perpetrator, instead of giving justice to the victim. Therefore, she was overcome by anxiety. That, however, was the prelude to the tsunami that was brewing in the wings of the wind—unbeknownst to her, this was just the first few steps in the order of battle.

...

Let's take an in-depth look at the big picture of war and the sequence of its operations and see how soldiers execute the order of battle or battle preparation drills.

Over the years the mechanics of fighting wars have acquired dramatic improvements. It has transitioned from sadistically charging with swords, spears, battering rams, and firing bow and arrows, to more potent, intelligent, and sophisticated methods.

These methods include weapons of mass destruction, smart bombing, shooting, nuclear gassing, biological, psychological warfare, use of drones, and to a lesser extent spiritual warfare. But in all cases the fundamentals are from the beginning, improving at every opportunity, but never changes.

Before soldiers go to war, they have drills that they observe;

these drills are referred to as the order of battle or battle preparation drills—it's like getting the materials and priming the walls of a house before painting; or making a budget prior to spending. It is a method in which they prepare for the eventualities to limit or minimize any unforeseen inconvenience or unfortunate surprises.

In the order of battle, soldiers prepare themselves and meticulously plan for the enemy and every possible outcome of the operation that they might be subjected to, so that they have a successful mission.

In this, the Support and Services contingent provides the clothing and equipment, food, transportation, weapons, and ammunition that the soldiers would need for the mission.

The soldiers would then carry out a personal inspection of their food and equipment to ensure that the food is fresh and the equipment sturdy and battle ready.

Their weapon type and cleaning equipment would be based on the ground, or area of fighting and climatic conditions. The soldiers would also pack dehydrated foods, and any gadget that would make them comfortable under adverse conditions.

Next, a section of this unit would form a secondary reconnaissance team for intelligence purposes as they would have already had intelligence report from people on the ground before the mission. The secondary reconnaissance team would spearhead the mission. They would gather more detailed information on the target using undetected stealth after which they would convey reports to the headquarters and to the unit in operation.

The necessary reports would include the enemies' grid reference or the ground which they occupy indicating whether it is open country or high ground (hillside). Reports would include the target's dress, their disguise, eating time, sleeping time, lifestyles, strengths and weaknesses, tactics, weaponry, and any other information that would aid to prepare tact against the enemy to ensure a successful mission.

Headquarters would then select the battalion, company or section needed for this operation, based on the size and potential of enemy indicated by this secondary intelligence unit.

The mission would then be outlined, and the soldiers briefed. Time would be synchronized. Methods of drop off and pick-ups would be discussed, signals platoon would relate the call signs, medics would be attached to the platoons, and then final checks revised.

After that is done, the soldiers would observe harboring drills. In this, they would occupy a piece of ground near drop-off point, and set up an all-round defense, or a perimeter guard if it is guerrilla warfare. If it is a conventional and urban area the methods vary but must be quick and decisive.

In the guerilla warfare, after the drop-off, the soldiers would form the all-round defense. This is a method by which each group of soldier assumes a position, or covers an arc of the area of occupation, then faces outward and visually comb their arc of occupation, to ensure the security of their immediate ground.

The commander would walk around tactically and release one out of every group to form a work routine. This work routine is a group that would dig latrines, set up a secondary headquarters and build bivouacs or tents to live in.

After they are settled in, they would withdraw the all-round defense, and post sentries who would guard at intervals throughout the entire occupancy, night and day.

From here, patrols would be sent out. The first patrol sent out would form an observation post. Again, this is another form of intelligence for message conveyance. In this, they would position themselves at a point where they can see the enemy's camp without being seen, and they can be in that position for days, to act as spies and watch the enemy's camp and report further development of the enemy position.

They would at no time engage the enemies in battle, as they would at all times remain hidden.

The water patrol is sent out next. They gather water for the team and would break their tracks when leaving or entering their campsite. They would not drop food items, wear cologne, or anything that the enemy could use to discover their position, or base.

Finally, the fighting patrols are sent out. Their purpose is to interrogate, antagonize, and injure the enemy to slow them down, and at times, kill the enemy, spoil them, destroy their radar nets, burn their villages, torture casualties for maps and information of other camps, or villages in close proximity. Then destroy the enemy's food supply, pollute their water, and sometimes burn the residue to the ground.

...

The soldiers, upon accomplishment of the mission, would reorganize, report details, and move on, on instructions from headquarters. When moving from point A to point B, tactics and camouflage are ensured and cannot be over-emphasized.

The soldier's dress must match the background he occupies. When traveling, no one soldier walks by himself; the least number of soldiers that walk, is a squad of five or seven.

During movements, the scout is always in front to scrutinize every detail and assess when movement is possible. During this period of movement from base to base, they travel in formations based on the ground they occupy, to protect themselves and ensure quick and effective reaction in case of attacks.

When they are traveling in narrow paths at nights, they are no more than three meters apart, or as close as possible that they can see the man in front, so no one would go missing without notice. They travel in arrowhead formation in open ground because this provides a type of all-round defense.

They also travel in single files or extended lines, and formation changes as they go along. During this period of traveling ambushes are set near water holes, or any place that would seem likely for the enemy to rest.

Before returning to base all these drills would be repeated in a sporadic manner until the mission is completed or headquarters stand down the operation. In any event, the mission would not be stood down before leaving permanent scars on the enemy.

After every operation, checks are done to see who is missing or injured. Treatment would be administered, and weapons would also be checked, and a fresh set of ammunition issued.

When attacking a camp, or when reacting to enemy forces, firefighting is done under control, on instructions from the team commander, to ensure precision and accuracy and to minimize casualty among themselves, this is also done to lessen the waste of ammunition.

...

In the believer's battle, the devils do the same in their onslaught as do the soldiers in a natural war. The devils will take days, weeks, or even months, spying and studying the believer before attacking; and if they find a door for entry, they will leave indelible impression if they get the chance to do so. That is to say, the order of battle and the entire battle preparation, planning, and execution of warfare have major similarities.

The major difference is that one is natural, affecting the spiritual, and the other is spiritual, affecting the natural.

Though the methods of preparation and planning are similar, the executions of the principles are different. In that, the soldiers physically occupy grounds based on the reconnaissance of men, but the believers battle must be fought in the spirit, and on the knees, or in whatever prayer position chosen, based on the instructions or reconnaissance of the Holy Spirit. Here, the believer will execute the same battle preparation drills that the soldiers did; only, it will be in the spirit.

Nevertheless, the believer, though potent, remains potential until he or she starts fasting and praying. And, when the believer prays, he or she must have the intelligence, the knowledge, and the understanding of what is happening as well as the purpose of what is happening—this is a sore point that even the scripture addresses, in that, God's people are destroyed because of lack of knowledge (Hosea. 4:6).

In this regard, for the believer to be successful, he or she must first find the mind of Christ. Finding the mind of God is finding the necessary knowledge, hence the purpose—this is so, in that, God will allow some things to prevail, so that other things might be resuscitated. And, if the believer does not know this, he or she will be wasting time praying for God to abort the process, not knowing, or understanding the mind of Christ.

In addition, the believer cannot be selfish, he or she must be Kingdom minded. In that, much of the prayers that are prayed, should be prayed on behalf of the people, the community, the province, or the state—and not just for the believer's individual purpose. Note that every action the soldiers carried out was for the team and ultimately the government that they served.

...

In the believer's battle, an effective method to execute the order of battle when praying, is to create a similitude or map of an image of the grounds of trial in the mind. This is what the soldiers do physically in harboring drills. They literally occupy the ground, create an all-round defense for protection and take charge of the grounds before sending out patrols. In like manner, if the believer can summon the mental fortitude to map the grid references and coordinates in the mind, and create a replica of the ground, then begin to pace that ground, or walk around the image of that area while praying, the believer has taken spiritual authority over the territory or stronghold (Jos. 1:3, 6. 1-27).

The ground paced or the area walked around represents and becomes the area of challenge. In so doing, the warrior has brought the actual grounds to his turf. For if in the mind, the battle can be mapped, faith can be invoked, and God be glorified. In that, God can and will do exceedingly, abundantly, above whatever one can ask or think and the battle is his (Eph 3:20).

To begin this kind of warfare, the believer's temple therefore must be prepared through confession, repentance, fasting and prayers, the washing and renewal of the Holy Spirit and an adequate diet of the word of God. This is the believer's method of packing hardware and making sure he or she is battle appropriate.

The intelligence that the believer possess involves the word of God and his spirit of discernment. This is analogous to the reconnaissance that the soldiers have in place. In that, with dreams and visions, instinct, and inspiration, the Lord reveals the areas necessary to approach at specific times. In this, God is in the spy-playing role discomfiting the enemy. Here knowledge is power, as the keen ear of the believer is briefed with all the information necessary to carry out the mission—an example of God fighting the battle for the believer and giving grid references and coordinates to the prophet can be found in 2 Kings 6:8 -10.

...

Unlike the soldier and demons with episodes of antagonistic attitude towards the opposition to get information, for intimidation, and to discomfit or plague them, the believer does not seek to directly confront the enemy; instead, the believer develops a relationship with God, and keep a constant interaction and fellowship with him, praying always in the spirit. Here, the emphasis is placed on what God is able to do and not what the devils can or have done. This, in itself, is a constant lethal torment to the devils.

Relationship with God is done through separation from sin, much prayer, the reading of his words, and fasting. Prayer—particularly that which is filled with the word, or promises of God—saturates the battleground, and as it intensifies, the angels excel in strength and are ready at a moment's notice to launch the attack and do the will of God (Ps. 103:20).

This order of battle is then intended to highlight the spiritual resemblance in Christian groundbreaking and taking back possession of what the enemy has stolen.

These same attitudes can be used to cast out demons or take back a city which the enemy has polluted. It is then important to first identify the enemy, be aware of the enemy's arsenal, strategize and position oneself to attack—here, emphasis should not be placed on the wiles of the devils; instead, the emphasis should be on putting on the whole armor of God (Eph 6:11-18).

At the same time, when preparing for battle, it is necessary to understand the types of devils involved in order to offend them effectively.

The knowledge that we wrestle not against flesh and blood but against principalities and powers and rulers of darkness of this world and spiritual wickedness in high places is a grand point to make one aware that the war is not only against delinquent perpetrators but against dignitaries and people of high rank and order. Hence, it would be wise not skip the formality of preliminaries.

Even though the battle is the Lord's, the believers play a vital role; hence, there are steps to be taken, principles to work with, and knowledge to understand.

When it comes to spiritual wickedness in high places, one must be reminded that it is a fact that demons have rank, intelligence, and personality.

In the ranks of demons there are princes ruling towns, cities, countries, and continents. The rank of the prince demon increases proportionally to the population of the domain in terms of commerce, occupants, and activities.

Their headquarters or domains are called stronghold, garrisons, and citadels—these are fortified concentrated units or areas. And, the approach to any of these domains must be mapped carefully when tackling any objective.

An example of a stronghold is as follows: If there is a town or community that is plagued with murderers, thieves, rapists, drugs smugglers and abusers, it means that the blood of those who are slain, are crying from the ground to be avenged, and will not rest until avenged; hence, blood touches blood. Therefore, the demons that are settled in that area will fortify their presence by attracting other spirits and as a result, the area becomes a stronghold (Num. 35:33-34, Gen.4:10, Deu. 32:43, Rev 6 :10).

Note too, that even though God governs in the affairs of men, he will not always intervene uninvited, because the earth was given to man to dress and to keep. Hence, if there is not an effective body of saints present to cry out to God for help, this demonic onslaught will assuredly escalate.

As a result of the blood pollution in the land caused by murderers, the presence of God, his blessing and help is withdrawn from the area and the prince demon and his host solidify their position—hence, the immorality escalates.

In this regard, the full force of the enemy is at work, which is to kill, to steal, and to destroy. For anywhere there are murderers, the robbers will be invited, and the spirit of the destroyer is attached to these two. That means, they will not stop at stealing and destroying your property, they will move on to rape, desecrate, intimidate, incarcerate, humiliate and devastate this community and its occupants—this is evidence of a stronghold. Notably enough, these devils attract a multitude of other spirits, especially the spirit of fear and intimidation.

...

In areas where the land is polluted, the first step in the believer's order of battle, is to pray for the mind of Christ so that he or she can have eyes to see, ears to hear, and a heart to understand the process needed to bind the strongman and spoil his goods. The strongman in this regard would be the prince of that area.

Hence when the shepherd is slain the sheep will scatter. Note carefully before we move on, that demons are disembodied spiritual beings with an intellect.

They have to possess people for their work to be of optimum effect. In this case, the people possessed are not necessarily limited to the murderers; but is an extension to the evil rulers or the hierarchy of that town that are involved. However, the most important thing to know is that somebody must carry the prince demon around.

...

If you recall the scriptures where there was a conspiracy against king David and he had to run for his life from his own son, Absalom, who partially overthrew him.

Absalom took counsel from his father's counselor, Ahithophel, who strengthened his hand against his father, the king. The Bible said Ahithophel's counsel was as if a man inquired at the oracle of God. That means that this man was one of credible status in God at that time, and highly influential towards the political arena—ironically, his name meant brother of ruin, or folly.

He turned against the ruling of God, and of David, and wanted to kill David. Being the chief campaigner for Absalom to be king, he became David's worst enemy (2 Sam.16-15-23. 17v1-4).

Now the same spirit of Lucifer was now working with this fellow—the spirit of betrayal, rebellion, undermining, mutiny, and murder—all these demons were wrapped up in the presence of this priest. Without second-guessing, you can already tell who was carrying the prince demon around.

Ahithophel was not fighting against David, because the scriptures says that the least you do unto one of these, you do it unto God; therefore, he was fighting against God. Absalom was just a figurehead walking in the counsel of the un-godly, waiting for a position that he could never have earned through just means. Ahithophel was the vein that pulled the trigger finger.

When king David heard that Ahithophel was among the conspirator, his prayer was constructed against the shepherd, which was Ahithophel in this case, because he was carrying around the prince demon. Therefore, David had the knowledge to ask God to confuse the counsel of Ahithophel (2sam 15v31). What this mean, is that, if the head is confused, his cohorts will scatter or become disoriented.

The point in this is that, sometimes, the prince can be carried around by the rulers of the city and not only the delinquents who are used as the executioners. Without the 'order of battle' or 'battle preparation drills' in which the reconnaissance is done, and the mind of Christ sought, none of the information given would be known to the believer.

Be not afraid nor dismayed by reason of this great multitude; for the battle is not yours, but God's.

2 Chronicles 20:15

Chapter Seven
The Battle Cry and Assault

The tension in the courtroom was more than I anticipated—it felt more like a ceremonial event rather than a trial. My aunties, uncles, grandmother, and dad were there with my mother. The buzz of whispering voices swelled into noisy chatter as people squeezed into the empty spaces of the tightly packed room. At the voice of the vertically challenged bailiff, the murmurs and chatter silenced giving way to his introduction of the case:

"The superior court of the state of New York is now in session. The County of New York. NY 214.... the people of New York vs. 'John Doe.' The Honorable Judge Samantha Black presiding. Please come to order."

Everyone seemed mechanical and tensed—caged behind wooden rails and square desks. The lawyers were on opposite sides of the room, jurors boxed to the side, and the Judge in the middle on an elevated podium. The only sound in the room was the rustle of papers on the prosecutor's desk.

The judge asked the prosecutor if the people was ready. He slid his chair back, stood up, buttoned his jacket and went forward to make his opening remarks—he approached the jury slowly, introduced himself, thanked them for answering the call to serve, and then made his appealed; telling them what they would be hearing, and pleaded to them that they should remain focused and vigilant regardless of the fog and theatrics. Telling them not to ignore the fact that the lives of multiple women were destroyed because of the harrowing and wretched experience, brought on by the heinous crimes of a man in whom the country had entrusted the responsibility to protect and to serve.

I sat two benches behind the prosecutor, angry at the calm demeanor of my assailant, yet curious to find out if the short row of women in front of me were the ones whom the prosecutor referred to in his opening remarks.

The defense lawyer came next, seemingly sober, and rather daring, practically vouched for the character of the assailant, noting that it would be beneath his moral ethics to represent a man of the alleged character if he had the slightest inclination that he was guilty; asking the jurors to look beyond the veil, examine the nuances, and lay the blame squarely at the feet where it belongs, less the blood of the innocent rests upon their shoulders.

One of the ladies who sat on the bench in front of me looked over her shoulder at me. She was weeping like a willow. When she looked around the second time, I almost fell off the bench in surprise and right there I realized that they were the ladies that the prosecutor was referring to in his opening statement. Though her swollen cheeks and puffy, red eyes somewhat disfigured her features, the memory of our meeting at the hospital and the connection we made, made it easy to use her bulgy eyes and trembling lips to recognize her—she was my Attending Nurse.

What was she doing here? I thought. *Didn't she say that she never reported the crime? How did the prosecutor find and linked her to this case? Was a forensic exam admissible after so many years?* My head began to spin.

It was as though the prosecutor brought all the weeping women to parade in front of the jury to make a statement and support his claims. Woman after woman testified of feeling lethargic and not having any memory of giving consent.

When the police officer, who had taken my statement, was called to the stand and was questioned, I sat at the edge of the bench and listened. I thought the prosecutor would have labored the point of inefficiency on the part of the police department concerning the so-called misplacement of the original testimony, but he glossed over the main points, ask trivial questions about the practice of evidence collection and moved on.

Medical reports were read, and DNA evidence were brought

into play. Medical experts and lab technicians were questioned by both the defense and the prosecutor about the nuances of the drug ketamine and others that were found in my stomach and that of the weeping women.

The prosecutor labored the point that the drug had dissociative and psychedelic properties and was given with intent, thus leading to the hallucination of the women, while the defense argued that the drug was an analgesic and an antidepressant—a simple pain killer that the women might have innocently taken for regular pains, or probably as a boost in the spirit of the party, since nobody actually witnessed anyone directly placing it in their drinks.

Gears shifted and the prosecutor had his moment—though at the end, the defense claimed it was speculative, he had a moment with the audience of the court. Members of the jury leaned forward when he presented a map that charted vicinities of ladies' homes, nearby bars, and a timeline of events that suggested that the perpetrator's whereabouts coincided with the whereabout of victims that were either assaulted or went missing. People sat on the edge of their benches; eyes fixed on the prosecutor.

I could tell that the prosecutor wanted to tag the assailant as a serial rapist. But to me, it was as though he went off on a tangent and lost the required focus and quintessence of the point needed to tie together the loose ends. It might have been a smarter move if he had capitalized solely on the weeping women whose testimonies he had.

Nevertheless, each time the defense lawyer hit the floor, he ripped through us women as though we were the wicked witches who violated the perpetrator—insinuating and at times outright saying that we were disgruntled one-night stands, and women of easy virtue.

The defense lawyer presented an immaculate military record of the assailant, his numerous tours in Afghanistan and Iraq, the lives he saved, the testimonies of his fellow soldiers, his contribution to the country and to his community, the relationship he has with his mother and sisters—the lawyer even brought up his fifth-grade school report, showing how much of a stellar student he was, and by doing so, pointing out the nature of his character from an early age, and how unseemly the allegations were.

It wasn't until the second day before I was made to take the stand. In my mind, that, in and of itself, was an embarrassment. The defense lawyer did not have elaborate questions to ask me. His tact was simple. He asked straightforward questions, at times requiring that I answered only yes, or no—questions such as the following: where do you live? Where were you the night before the incident? Did you have friends at the party? Can you say how many of your colleagues were there that night? How familiar are you with that restaurant?

He then addressed the judge, made a statement about admitting a piece of evidence, then nodded to a court attendee who then proceeded to set up a video on the dusty television towards the front of the courthouse. I immediately noticed that the video was taken from the bar that we were at that fateful night. The defense fast-forwarded the video to where I was casually walking over to my assailant who was sitting by himself having a drink.

Though the audio could not be heard, the video showed us having drinks, laughing, chatting, and me acting like the flirt I was that night. He then paused the video and asked if I recognized any of the persons in the video. When I answered yes, he pointed his infrared pointer at myself and the assailant and asked if I recognized the images. He then played the video and paused it at a point where I flung my head back with laughter. Leaving that image on the screen, he timely asked me if at any time up to that point I felt threatened or uncomfortable—or if I was coerced to have a seat and be engaged in the conversation. And, if there were any signs of manipulation of will.

He paused between each question and waited for my response, leaving the picture on the screen as if he wanted to use the picture as a reminder that I was having fun. When I answered no, to each portion of his questions, he continued along that line—playing the video, pausing, and asking questions.

He then fast-forwarded the video to the point where my assailant and I were leaving the bar. My arm over his shoulder, his hands around my hip. The defense then turned to the jury and pointed at the video, stating that there were no signs of force, coercion, or manipulation of will. Mentioning that those were my words when he questioned me earlier. Then he rewinds the video to one of my flirtatious moments where I had my hand on my assailant's arm and paused it there. He then turned to me and asked if I had known his client prior to that night. When I answered no, he asked me how comfortable I was when I kept touching his client—before I could answer, he moved to the next question as though the first was unimportant, or as if it was rhetorical. He asked how often I went drinking and how often I met with strangers at bars—

Though at intervals the prosecutor tried to point out that the questions were leading, argumentative, and irrelevant, the judge gave the defense the latitude—an opportunity the defense took, using words like alluring, coy, sensual, and seducing, to describe my flirtatious gesticulations, painting me as a common whore before my family, and possibly in the minds of the jurors without actually calling me a whore.

My grandmother looked at me with what seemed like a blend of disgust and pity. The sounds in the video came on muffled then diminished and still nobody could distinguish what my colleague and I were saying when I was leaving the bar, and so the defense lawyer had a field day—asking what in that video suggested force, where in that video are the signs of coercion, and does the visual evidence lie?

The members of the jury were silent, head steady, eyes focused, noting his every clause, his every enunciation—they learned in even when he paused, and listened attentively.

It was not in my best interest to sit through the agitation and mental devastation brought on by my disappointment in the inept prosecutor. I left that day with no intention to return. The case continued for the next two days and took just a few hours for the jury to deliberate.

In any event, all I needed to hear was the outcome. All I wanted was justice to be served. Nevertheless, from what I saw the first day, I knew the prosecuting lawyer was no match for the defense—the defense was like a sophist—he was witty with words; he twisted the facts and took the lesser argument and made it into a more logical appeal than the truth. And, while trampling the prosecutor's arguments, he discredited every one of the weeping women and made their testimonies seem worthless.

Though I stayed home, my aunties never missed a session. They monitored the proceedings meticulously and came home each day with different degrees of disappointments and aggression as though they too were victims that begged for restitution or reparation.

My mother and grandmother stayed with me at home, counseling every chance they got as though I was in therapy.

At the end of the trial my aunties told us the verdict without saying what the verdict was—they fussed with each other and argued back and forth as they stepped from the car.

"How could he?"

"Could there have been a sillier closing argument?" one said.

"Doesn't he know that he must remind the jury of the devastation periodically to keep the most tragic experience fresh on their minds?" said the other.

"What kind of stupid prosecutor was that?"

"I wonder if the defense approached him and paid him off, secretly?" one asked, and they looked at each other questioningly.

When they came into the house, they hugged and held me as though they were the hypothetical firewall against the anguish and distress that emerged in the pit of my stomach. But all I felt was the defeat, the disappointment, and the despondency that accompanied loss. Yet, they held me. Care and concern were wrapped in every pulsating heartbeat—but all I saw was the darkness that had descended, the darkness that engulfed and transported me listlessly to a silent place, a lifeless land steaming with asphalt, dead trees, burnt buildings, and smog.

I held my throat and gasped.

Yet, they held me.

ears ran down my face as did theirs, and in that moment of self loathe, I felt as though nothing—except the victory that I didn't receive—could restore the pride, the poise, and the prissiness of my character that had been ripped from my spirit the night I escaped the snare of my attacker.

All I could think about were the headlines of the publication that would probably be in the local papers the next day. The headlines that would be archived in the public's minds for the rest of their days—not tucked away neatly in obscurity, but in the prefrontal cortex of everyone's brain.

Wars are usually fought for territories, economic resources, and ideology. The war that the believer is engaged in is a war for souls. In that regard, if the devils can control the territories, the resources, and the ideology, then they are in position to capitalize on and ultimately win the souls of men.

Souls belong to God, and it is not his will that any should be lost; nevertheless, man has a will and is able to make choices and there is a Devil whose job is to kill, to steal, and to destroy.

However, regardless of the enemy's job titles, God gave man authority and dominion over everything in the air, the land, and the sea—that is, over territories, resources, and ideology (Ps. 8:6-8, Gen. 1:26).

Since the believer has authority over territories, resources, and can control the narrative concerning ideology, the believer is a direct threat to the devils' plan. That is to say, when the believer is in alignment with God's plan to ensure that his glory covers the earth, that puts the believer at war with the devils.

Though many believers are aware of the war that they are engaged in, it is as though they are not fully aware of the power that they wield. It has become a cliché in church circles, but is a fact, that one believer can chase up to a thousand demons all by him or herself, and if two believers join forces, they can chase away up to ten thousand demons (Deu. 32:30, Jos. 23:10).

When it comes to the more powerful demons, such as prince demons that rule over cities and towns, the believer is equipped with power that supersedes every power of those demons—that is, power to bind kings with chains and nobles with fetters of iron (Ps. 149: 6-9, Acts 1:8, Matt. 18:18-20).

Nevertheless, though the believer is equipped to out maneuver the devils, this is war, though the devils know that they have the losing hand, and a short time, they will not roll over and play dead—they will antagonize, infiltrate, and create doors so that the believer who does not have the knowledge of his or her purpose, and power, will cower before them. The scripture states that he is like a roaring lion, walking about, seeking whom he may devour (1Pet 5:8).

In other words, it is the devils' desire is to sift the believer and keep him or her in a place of inability and lack so that the believer does not fulfill his or her purpose (Luke 22:31).

Therefore, we can safely say then that whenever a believer is positioned to do great exploits, devils are assigned to destroy that believer from the inception.

Jasmine was not an exception to that rule. It is the devil's job to kill, to steal, and to destroy, while it is the believer's job to stand against the wiles of the devil.

Jasmine's psychological war is not different from any other wars that believers are engaged in.

War is war.

In that regard, the preliminaries are not any different from what takes place in a courtroom; neither are they any different from the negotiations that take place before a war. Every war starts with a defense and a prosecutor. Two opposing forces vying for dominance, gathering information and doing whatever it takes to get the upper hand. Putting forth their best argument to convince themselves, or a certain group, or even the masses who would pass judgement based on the more convincing argument and not necessarily the truth.

...

War is war.

In cases of large-scale operations against countries with strong backbone, connection to allied forces, optimum military power, large population, and valuable economic resources, spies are sent in as normal, and they would channel reports to their headquarters who in turn would release that information to the government. Upon receiving this information, the aggressor would, through craft, pretend to exhaust every diplomatic relation to arrive at a compromise. At the same time, the aggressor would ensure that the so-called compromise would be unreasonable and unacceptable to the opposition—more like, to provoke and anger them.

Further proposals would be made to get the opponent to comply with reasons; offers would be discussed in terms of bribes or payoffs. Then if nothing turns, the usual case of a disastrous rumor would be fabricated to earn foreign support.

Sometimes the very aggressor and the opponent are not the real reason for the impending war, but a manipulative external source that would profit.

War would then be inevitable, unless the opponent wishes to become the aggressor's slave and puppet, which in most cases are not likely; hence, the political part of the war starts first. In that, support groups and foreign aids are cut off in a sudden rippling manner, and economic sanctions are imposed.

Whenever a country is under sanction, the aggressor, in order to cripple and deteriorate the economy of the opposition over a period, can use time as a tool. Time however, if not managed wisely, can affect both the defender as well as the aggressor because the business of war is very expensive.

However, depending on the strength, resources, and ability of the opposition to bounce back, everything is best done rapidly. In this, it is necessary to attack and do so quickly by air, from which they bomb the entry and exits to the enemy's oil plants and supplies, railways, and airstrips. They would dig ditches in roadways and send in soldiers to seize bridges that are en-route to objectives and damage those that are not.

And, since wars are handled as a business, there are certain infrastructures and resources that are carefully safeguarded by the attacker to obtain spoils.

Therefore, damage would be administered under control to protect specific facilities especially reservoirs, barges, food and supply factories. Nevertheless, the enemy would plant mines in its rival's waters, shoot down airborne planes, destroy their media and cut off their communications from the rest the world.

Time is allowed once more for the damage to take effect and as the opposition supplies ran out, the process of intimidation and frustration is repeated.

When the nourishment and internal-dependence or self-sufficiency of the country has totally collapse and the people are weakened physically, mentally, and psychologically, the armored divisions followed by the ground troops would be sent in to inhabit and wipe out any other pockets of resistance, mop up, and take over.

At times the allied forces may assist, and then you could say, it is one country against the world.

Even though there are supposedly rules that govern these kinds of wars, on the actual battlefield the rule is, 'there are no rules' it is by any means necessary to obtain the objective: wearing the enemy's uniform to lure them into traps, using ambulances to transport troops instead of sick and medication, raising the enemy's flag to make-belief that they have control and drop arms as they enter campsite, are just a few of the different strategies to the kill.

War is mean, destructive, devastating, disastrous, and corrupt. Both parties involved are apt to suffer and undergo losses. Many never return to their port of embarkation.

Those who survive are maimed by the scars of battle with missing limbs, battle shock and nerve loss, and the never fading picture of the grim details from the scenes of battle.

The recipient countries of this terrible misfortune are left in the most deplorable state: spiritually, physically, and psychologically. Children, as well as adults die, homes are destroyed; schools, churches, hospitals, and every supposedly occupied structure are burned and destroyed.

Time at war impacts infrastructure. In the absence of maintenance, structures begin to deteriorate. Water mains are broken, and waters are polluted. Sewage mains break and coagulate spreading all types of communicable diseases.

The unbearable stench of improperly disposed bodies and sewage-remains goes up, as do the smoke of the burning furnaces of buildings.

By this time, mobility ceases, electricity fails, and the only light is that of the sun by day, and the glare of fire by night.

As darkness takes its toll to add to the anguish, starvation sets in, and further frustration surmounts. The wounded die, the morgues fill up, the grieving undertakers—if it had not been war—would be otherwise financially blessed, and the country becomes a big graveyard.

After any such devastation, if the attacker's plan was just to kill, steal, destroy, and not to inhabit permanently, then would caring neighboring countries send in relief items such as medication, water, food, tents flashlight and other necessary gadgets by air drop off.

If the attackers inhabit the land and set up their own interim government, then the neighbors would have to fight for the country's release.

If it was a case where the allied forces are against this country, habitation would continue until they are sure that that country is not a threat to the system and their society. Then it will take some unions or federation, or even the media to begin to hit against the operation for them to withdraw.

The results are usually the same after every war; that is, massive rebuilding is necessary. Relief programs would be activated, engineers from foreign countries would be sent to clear drains, rebuild bridges, mend airstrips, and defuse mines and such the like. The injured country usually takes years to rebuild its economy, and when it does, it is closely monitored by the adversary, in case the rulers should plan to hit back.

...

What started out as a natural feeling to satisfy a youthful desire in Jasmine's life metastasized into a dilemma that now affects her psychologically. The unexpected outcome of events pushed her into a state in which she subconsciously cocooned herself into a world of depression that none of her aunties could understand.

Though the aunties represented a strong backbone in Jasmine's life, and though her mother might be able to provide psychological help to some degree, her injuries would take more that the works of the apothecary for her to heal. This family needed an intervention, this family needed the remedy that Jesus gave the disciples—they needed to fast and to pray.

The scripture states that the disciples of Jesus once had difficulties delivering a child; Jesus told them that the reason they failed was because of their lack of faith and belief. He went on further to explain to them that if they had faith like a mustard seed, they could do mighty deeds; however, the kind of deliverance that the child needed, could not be done through faith, only—it could only be done through prayer and fasting (Matt. 17:14-21).

...

If we should look at the pattern of demonic attacks on the believer, it would become evident that the pattern is like that of the soldiers in their battle preparation. The styles and tactics that the devil uses are the same as soldiers on the battlefield. And the devils aim is to kill, to steal, and to destroy.

Therefore, please, do not encourage sin.

My grandmother—God bless her soul—used to tell me that, 'devils find work for idle hands' I took that to believe that as becoming believers, one should always make him or herself busy with the things of God; otherwise, boredom will cause a craving for the things that wars against the spirit.

Jasmine, wanting to free herself from the demands of study, instead of attaching herself to a spiritual base, something that is bigger than herself, she sought to satisfy the desires of the flesh with any available companion, and a party.

In other words, it is best not to make choices base on the dictates of feelings—feelings will change, but the facts will remain; therefore, do not compromise. Do not bargain with devils. Resist the feeling, the unction, and the need, and it will flee from you, and by so doing, shun the very appearance of evil. Remember also, that the devil can transform himself into an angel of light, so do not be fooled by the things that seem harmless, do not be attracted to everything that glitters—it's not always gold. Try the spirits to see if they are of God.

...

Let me hurry to say that nobody is beyond the scope of the devils' attack. In that regard, when the deeds of humble people catch God's attention through worship like Cornelius, praise like David, youthful innocence like Samuel and Solomon, or even in humility like the woman of Samaria—God then sees potential and decides to make good of such.

The devils also notice potential in people, and become jealous, which is what they always do, unless God shield their eyes, which I believe is unlikely, because here is where the stage is set for the believer to grow in God and to help others through his or her testimony.

This is the time when value is added to the believer's life. And, we all know that the Lord would never give a promotion without first training the believer for the position.

Here, the devils, whose job is the accuser of the brethren, would do everything to prove to God that the believer is not deserving. In their bid to deflect the purpose of God, they would send out spies to judge and test character, spirituality, influence, firmness and the faith in God of the chosen individual.

The devils would then plant obstacles in place to start the process of mental interrogation. The reason for this is that if they can get the believer to fall into depression and lose focus and become distracted, then they would have stopped a future destruction to their camp. If they succeed at this point, they will go in for the kill, causing the party involved to abort the God intended process; hence, becoming dormant and dying naturally—a spiritual death.

It is at this point that demons intercept and try to kill seeds. In that, they influence people to cut off all support. They put enmity amongst family members, drive wedges into that which is supposed to be closely knitted, and shun friends and associates through heresy, discord, rumors, resentment, and malice.

Then, arranged circumstances would arise to deplete the finances through a rippling effect, that when accrued, would engulf every asset; as a result, the once kindhearted burden bearing and sharing associates-business relationships, would transform into a wild safari of hunter and prey.

Time in these situations would be a most devastating tool used to encourage depression and insanity. To make matters worse, this peril would be repeated until nakedness and famine are ensured.

Then the ground troops that would take over and inhabit; in that, it is now the people or close friends who would prepare the platform of criticism and scorn—lighting the fire of discord, which would spread like a cancer polluting even the innocent, who in turn, would fan the flames through heresy.

Sickness would be somewhat inevitable in some sense and the rebirth of the life and suffering of the prophet Job is then highlighted, plunging the individual in a state of leprosy. Here, it can be then said that such an individual is being aborted from society and therefore deprived of the pacifiers of life. This is the result of an embargo of spiritual forces operating in the physical.

...

Here is a message to the believers: Though the vision tarry, wait for it. Do not curse God and die. Wait until your change comes. This is so because after being on the battlefield for an extended period, the demons of fear will be strengthened, insecurity will loom into greatness, unbelief, confusion, and doubt will pressure the mind, depression will be at its peak, spreading gloom and darkness into every recess that can be opened for light.

It is interesting however, that the Lord never gives a believer more than he or she can bear. And, with ever temptation, a way of escape is always being prepared.

Therefore, in this matrix of spiritual interferences, the only escape route is through praise, prayer, fasting, and the word of God. Weak men die in this war, likewise the strong, and those who made it out alive is either better or bitter; because it is in these tribulations that patience is birth and allowed to have her perfect way.

Here is where muscles gain lean and hands callous; the vessels become that of gold and silver and of honor. Impurities are burned out, and what was once cast-iron will become malleable, humility will be earned and faith in God is learned.

It is in the failure of these tests that hinders the anointing; hence, there are a lot of should-be pastors sitting in pews, being travel agents who can only point out destinations and never being able to become a tour guide.

Many Evangelists are imprisoned by unfortunate circumstances, and are joining the prayer lines consistently, asking for prayers instead of standing in faith and praying for the masses. To this kind of calamity, Solomon says, there is a vanity that is in the land, servants are on horses and sons are slaves (Eccles. 10:7).

It is unfortunate when prayer warriors who are supposed to be mounting up as eagles, are walking like chickens, and not being able to test the strength and tenacity of their wings. Many are maimed with scars of battle, harboring insecurity and fears, bondage in doubt, tongue tied with dumb spirits and having their vison blurred, packed with potential that cannot be kinetic.

Then the spirit of envy and covetousness looms among these believers as their juniors take the mantle and run in the race that they have abandoned, disregarding the shame of their cross.

The key to deliver oneself from this calamity is to know that, though a person has lost a few battles, he or she can still win the war. The key is to know that there is always hope and healing is in the house, because Jesus came to set the captives free; Jesus came to set at liberty them that are bruised and to preach the acceptable year of the lord. He came to give life and that more abundantly (Luke. 4:18-19, John. 10:10).

Hence, there are always fresh opportunities, the doors to the anointing are always opened even though the challenges become tougher with time. It is in this regard that God says, young man I call upon you because you are strong (1John 2:14).

Therefore, if you are hurt or hurting, don't just stay there and die quietly beneath the rubble. Forsake pride and let your weak and painful screams of agony and torment be heard, the rescuers and medics are nearby.

Look for the opportunity, create the play, make the tackle and fight from the offensive, put aside pride, reluctance, and the feeling of inferiority.

In war, casualties are inevitable, and the anointing has a price tag to it. It is said that the more a soldier sweats in training, the less he bleeds in war, but I say again, in war, casualties are inevitable; therefore, cry out for your foreign aid, if necessary.

There is room at the cross for you, there is healing in the house for you, the angel has touched and troubled the water, step right in and if you can't step in, just touch the hem of his garment with your prayers and praise.

Saying all of this to say, get over the grim details of battle, take off the grave cloth. Whatever is of good report, if there be any virtue, if there be any praise, think on those things (Phil. 4:8).

Get relief supply if necessary; clear the drains in your life that have been clogged by debris to cause over flooding. Rebuild the bridges that have been broken in battle. Pour fresh oil in your wounds; rekindle the spiritual fire. Break the curses, press on, press on, press on, cross over this your Jordan. Slay your Goliath, go back to your Bethel, speak to your rock, gird up your loins, put on your strength no matter how hard it gets. All you have to lose is a little sweat, a little tear, a little weight (and that's all liquid anyway), and it is good for the physical body—ask your local doctor.

Chapter Eight
Impact

My mother, having a spiritual upbringing, and being a psychologist, intuitively understood when her voice was irrelevant and when the voice of God was needed. And, though I fought tooth and nail against her ideologies and preferred to listen to my aunties, probably because they were the firecrackers who fiercely challenged every opposition and defended the family, I must confess that my mother was the deeper voice of reason. Her input was always final. Though she gave everyone leverage, when she spoke, nobody second guessed. Her advice was followed.

I suppose she noticed the wall that I barricaded myself behind and noticed how wrapped up I was in depression; therefore, she never approached me the way my aunts did, she dropped her words and left.

She gave me a scripture and suggested that I read it daily, but not before telling me about her experience on a trip to Jamaica where she got stuck for a lengthy period of time. Her story is as follows:

I have had the unfortunate privilege to experience Hurricane Gilbert in Jamaica, in 1988. What started out as a cool overcast day, was soon to become a picture of devastation, gloom, and despair. Not that it was without warning, because the weather forecasters and meteorologists had already given the early warnings, and people throughout the entire country had stocked their necessities and had batten down for the expected eventualities.

But the natives were soon to realize that their prior preparation was of little or no match to this formidable foe moving at 115-140 mph, hissing, hurling, and plundering in its rage, leaving behind a path of death, damage, and disease.

The hurricane tested and stretched the tenacity of every single person in the country. There were massive landslides, flooded lands; broken bridges, electrical failure, broken water mains, and many buildings lay in ruinous heaps.

Food became a scarce commodity, and except canned goods, the little we had was spoilt. Roads were blocked as a result of collapsed bridges and the landslides. The makeshift shelters were packed out, hospitals were full, 26 people were killed and over 500,000 people were left homeless—this is from a population of 2.5 million.

In the same breath, the bandits were merciless and had a field day looting and vandalizing, because the security forces had to make the choice of saving lives rather than to securing property—scrambling for their own lives and that of those that were in danger.

This was a time of peril in the country, and it brought everyone together to stand against the one common enemy.

The devastation made international headlines, and as a result, caring neighboring and foreign countries were quick to respond; they sent in relief items such as food, medication, and every essential requirement for rebuilding.

I can personally attest to the fact that out of the stench of that ruin came a glorious resurrection. In that, even though there were temporary setbacks in national development and standard of life, agriculture, transportation, power and communication, a more secured infrastructure was put in place overtime to face future eventualities. Foreign relationships and diplomatic ties grew stronger as everyone chimed in and supported the cause. It was a national crisis that gained international attention. The local natives of the suburbs got better roads and utilities and many of those who became homeless ended up getting better houses than that which they had before—I guess, what was intended for evil, worked out for good.

My mother was not one to be frivolous with matters she discussed. And, though at times I resented her stories, I must confess that every one of her stories were attached to a specific premise and had a particular purpose. But this one really struck a chord in my spirit, and so I ruminated on the possible meanings of every part. I knew that her anecdote was an allegory, and I knew exactly what she was saying. Simply put, she was saying, 'help is here, if you need it.' And, with that, I knew what I had to do.

Therefore, the next day, I decided to pray again, this time, I took up her postcard, unlatched the bow, read, and internalized the verses that she prescribed. As I read, I began to feel at ease, I began to feel a calm, I began to feel a release, and so I kept reading. It never struck me as any of the affirmations that I usually read; it didn't feel like a motivational speech, yet each word felt personal, it was as though each word reverberated in my spirit and before I knew it, I was in tears, uncontrollable tears—and, through water-logged eyes, I read it again, and again.

Overtime, it became a habit for me to read the scriptures, but that verse that my mother gave me, became my go-to verse. I ended up framing and keeping it in my room, it reads as follows: Awake, awake, put on thy strength, O Zion; put on thy beautiful garments, O Jerusalem, the holy city; for henceforth there shall no more come into thee the uncircumcised and the unclean. Shake thyself from the dust; arise, sit down, O Jerusalem; loose thyself from the bands of thy neck, O captive daughter of Zion (Isa. 52:1-2).

Stand still, and see the salvation of the Lord, which he will show you today; for the Egyptians whom ye have seen today, ye shall see them no more for ever.

Exodus 14:13

War has been declared upon the entire human race since the Devil and his hosts were cast out of heaven. In Adam's fall, all had fallen, because the whole human race was in his loins. The implications of Adam's fall are evident throughout generations; whether the circumstances are natural disasters, ethnic cleansing, or down right crime, every aspect, issues, and tendency of life is either for God to be glorified, or it is as a result of the impact of sinful spiritual influences and occurrences.

During the time when David was king of Israel, there was a grievous famine in the land for three years. Therefore, David prayed and asked God why, and the Lord told him that it was as a result of the injustices that the house of Saul did to the Gibeonites. David had to call a meeting with the Gibeonites to make reparations on behalf of the nation, and when they refused to accept monetary compensation, David had to grant them the lives of seven descendants of the perpetrator for the famine to be stopped (2 Sam 21).

In our society today and even in our personal lives there is war, it does not matter how much we give a blind eye, we must call a spade a spade, for the battle is raging. The moral values and our standard of living have drastically declined, what was once wrong, our constitution has transformed and made right.

The Bible is no longer in our schools, but the guns are. The youth and the elderly have plunge into sodomy, prostitution, pornography, witchcraft, and idolatry. Hence devils from the pit of hell are released in our society. Everyday the stories of war loom on our horizon; the number of crimes that are committed daily are unheard of. We have gone away from the ordinances of God and have sinned a great sin—hence, the land is polluted.

Therefore, we need Godly men and women to lead us back to the God of heaven. Men who will let their voices be heard, men who are not afraid of the repercussions, men who will not bow to the system of evil, regardless of situation, irrespective of conditions, and in spite of cause. We need men, young men who will turn their pots down, put on sackcloth and ash and cry out to God. We need Jesus, our nations need the Lord.

Hurricane Gilbert that Jasmine's mother used as her analogy had to be faced head on. The soldiers and rescue workers had to ignore their own families and their personal needs and respond to their assignments. They were under the orders of the government and had to work for the cause of the country—they had a calling to fulfill, something that was bigger than themselves.

The hurricane could not be fought with physical hands, and the people were intelligent enough to know that; therefore, they effectively did their part to assist with transportation, food, shelter, and the basic necessities, and left the rest to the mercies of God.

...

In that regard, we as believers have a commission from God and a part to play in spearheading repentance to divert this onslaught of evil across our nation. The results of sin have directly impacted our land. We have been hit from every angle and are troubled on every side, we must retaliate and face it head on. Now is not the time for pity parties and small talks, it's not the time to point finger in blame, the damage is already done, and all are affected.

Let us therefore humble ourselves, consider the region that God has placed us and repent on behalf of that region. Let us take stock and turn from our wicked ways. Let us fast, pray, and praise the God of heaven until he heals our land, until the earth gives its increase, and until God blesses us. What has gone bitter will become better—and we will rise triumphantly from the ashes.

Chapter Nine
Pressing Towards the Mark

Since my mother gave me that scripture and downloaded her Hurricane Gilbert analogy in my spirit, I became more aware of the world around me and more accountable for my actions. I still enjoyed the splendors of life, but I was more selective with my priorities—I gave myself to the reading of the word of the Lord, prayed more than I used to, and even went on the occasional fast. Truth be told, for me, it was a form of therapy. There were times when I knew that the Lord was leading me and using scriptures to comfort and restore me, and there were times when I was just finding scriptures that resembled my experience to prove to myself that anyone could have experienced the misfortune that I had encountered.

It wasn't until I came across the eventualities of the apostle Paul, that I realized the depth of suffering that believers undergo for the cause of Christ. I was dumbfounded when I stumbled on the revelation. Though a part of me felt that his dilemma was payback for the wrongs he did before his conversion, I still could not believe that one person would be willing to endure so much for a cause and remain on the path. It was astounding!

Nevertheless, when I read that he suffered for Christ's sake, I came to new levels of understanding. The scripture stated that '... *in prison more frequent, in deaths oft. Of the Jews five times received I forty stripes save one. Thrice was I beaten with rods, once was I stoned, thrice I suffered shipwreck, a night and a day have I been in the deep; in journeyings often, in perils of waters, in perils of robbers, in perils of mine own countrymen, in perils by the heathen, in perils in the city, in perils in the wilderness, in perils in the sea, in perils among false brethren; in weariness and painfulness, in watching often, in hunger and thirst, in fasting often, in cold and nakedness'* (2corinthians11: 23 – 27).

I read this text several times, each time trying to justify the cause. Questioning whether his misfortunes were the result of sin or for God to be glorified.

When I eventually moved on and read a little more of his writings, I realized that there is a place in God that every believer should endeavor to reach.

In his is writings, Paul said, *'I press towards the mark for the prize of the high calling of God, in Christ Jesus', and 'oh, that I may know him and the power of his resurrection and the fellowship of his suffering.'* (Philippians 3:1-14).

When I read that scripture, reviewed the life of Paul before he met Christ, looked at his secular lifestyle, his customs, his conversion after he met Christ, and his belief for future hope of glory, I got immense clarity, not only to his purpose, but to my purpose in the earth. I then understood the scripture that says, if we suffer with Christ, we shall also reign with him (2 Tim. 2:12). And that the sufferings of this present time are not worthy to be compared with the glory which shall be revealed in us (Rom.8:18).

Here is a prominent man of society, highly educated in the secular world and in the laws of Jewish customs, having infallible zeal, yet count all but loss for the excellency of the knowledge of Christ. Paul found out the purpose of human life on earth and was willing to give up all for that abundant life. Apart from Christ himself, Paul instantly became my mentor, and I, his protégé.

I found out too, that when the believer reaches "that place" in Christ, where the focus is on Jesus, regardless of the tribulations he or she endures, the believer becomes a powerful force of reckoning.

I then began to question my new knowledge, as to what is that hypothetical "mark" that Paul spoke of, and where is that "place." Asking myself questions such as: how does one get to that place, and what takes place in the process of getting there?

In my search, I found out that to sin, is to miss the mark.

Therefore, the mark must be steadfastness on the pathway that leads to eternal life regardless of circumstances.

The place is in Christ, for everyone that is in Christ has become a new creature. With that, I believe I would get there through humility, acceptance of who I am as a person, and to be honest with myself and with God, regardless of the trials and temptation I encountered.

I found out too, that as a believer, I do not belong to this world. My citizenship is of another country. As a result, I am an ambassador, a foreigner, a sojourner, a missionary, and a disciple.

I then understood that I was from a world govern by precepts and principles of righteousness. And, that my presence in this natural world, is a personification of a heavenly being. When I got this revelation as a believer, I found my true self. Through this type of identity, all obstacles pale into insignificance and a lifestyle of dominion was birth.

Therefore, when I stumbled upon this revelation and the scales of my vision were shed, the understanding of Christ took on a new meaning and left an indelible mark on me.

From then on, whatsoever decisions I made, whatsoever steps I took, had to be as a result of my knowledge, trust, dependability, and faith in Christ. I realized that every obstacle was just another hurdle aimed to prepare me for a greater purpose. I realized that though I might be troubled on every side, I was not destroyed. I realized that I was a problem for the devils as becoming an heir of Christ; therefore, I pressed towards the mark for the prize of the high calling, which is in Christ Jesus.

Forgetting those things which are behind, and reaching forth unto those things which are before, I press towards the mark for the prize of the high calling of God in Christ Jesus.

Philippians 3:13 - 14

The revelations that Jasmine had, as well as her new perspective on life, suggested that she has evolved to a new level of maturity. If you listen to her carefully, you will probably notice a bit of arrogance that borders on self-righteousness, you might also notice the zeal that she possesses, you will even notice where she speaks as though she had gathered experience through time spent in scriptures, so much so, that she might be able to explicitly explain them to someone, successfully.

Jasmine's realization is a shared experience amongst believers who fell in love with Jesus and spent quality time with him after their initial conversion. In the book of Revelation, the scripture refers to this as a person's 'first love' with Christ (Rev. 2:4-5).

This is the time in the believer's life when he or she wants everyone to be saved. This is the time when the believer wants God to return immediately. The change she experienced is the renewal of the mind that the scripture talks about.

It is interesting to note, as Jasmine alluded before she ended her story, that the mind of the believer is trained through trials, in the same manner that the refiner uses fire as a gold purifier. Withstanding trials and temptations usually determine how effective and efficient a believer becomes.

Note though, that the more effective or anointed the believer becomes, the more the number and rank of the devils that will attack, will increase. For example, if society has a problem with one delinquent or terrorist, and the army gets involved, the army will send out a section of fighting men to bring in that person; that is, if the person is not connected to a larger body of delinquents. Note here that a section consists of eight soldiers.

If there were a section of delinquents, the army would send out a platoon of fighting men against them to accost them—a platoon consists of at least thirty-two soldiers.

If there is a platoon of delinquents, then the army will send a company of soldiers against them—here, a company is made up of three platoons.

And, if a company of men makes themselves the enemy, the army will send out a battalion, and this consists of six companies.

These numbers given, are merely the skeleton amount as the bigger the army the numbers may differ. For instance, in the Roman army at the time of Jesus, they had large groups called legions and a legion would represent three to six thousand soldiers.

In this wise, if the believer continues to jump the hurdles and overcome the obstacles, the devil will multiply the enemies and send more and more devils against the believer. In other words, an entire host of demons can be unleashed upon the believer.

Nevertheless, as Jesus said to Peter, 'Peter, the devil desires to have you, that he might sift you as wheat, but I have prayed for you that your faith fail not' (Luke 22:31-32).

Interestingly, these evil agents never learn from seeing how the Lord works. Over and over again, what the devil has intended for evil, the Lord uses it for his good. At times, the situations are so complex and seemingly inescapable, but in those cases, the deliverance is utmost intriguing. In that, God uses the plots of the enemy to elevate, to train, and to deliver his people.

...

A prime example of how God uses the traps that the enemy has set to elevate, train, and deliver his people can be seen in the birth of Moses. The king of Egypt, through fear of being overthrown, thought that the Israelites were multiplying too fast; he therefore sought terminal measures from the midwives, unsuccessfully.

He then joined league with the people of his province to kill and throw every male child, two years and under, into the river. Whatever instinct or spiritual insight that caused Moses' mother to throw Moses in an ark, into the same destiny as the enemy would have, even among the dead in the river, was the same measure God used for his deliverance. Interestingly, not only his deliverance, but also passage that would enable him to enter, grow, get educated, and trained in the leadership principles of kings, first-hand, in the king's palace; ironically, with the same king that wanted him dead. God's ways are pass finding out. God's people go from the "mark" to the "place" through trials and tribulation so that only God can get the glory.

...

Every trial is an opportunity for increased spiritual growth—whether new or repeated—and, if the trial is repeated, that means that there is a test to pass or a new lesson to learn. More importantly, it could be a result of victories the believer has had in a previous battle and the enemy wants to overshadow the victory with doubt and despair. Or, it might be the gap that the believer is standing in for a fellow comrade. Whatever is the cause, humility must be exercised; in that, the outcome is not measured by the severity of the trial, but by the attitude taken therein. Therefore, the attitude determines the time spent circling the wilderness, or the time spent circling Jericho's wall.

...

Job was once such a man that the devil hit from land, sea and air. While his children faced their brutal death at the hands of the enemy, instantaneously his cattle were stolen, and his cattlemen perished by the sword. Without time to exhale, the news came that the fire of God has burned and killed his sheep and servants. In the same breath, the striking news of the death of his camels and servants. Then in the process of time sores on his body rotted. The hit and impact that he received was sudden, overwhelming, and excruciating.

We are used to go from rags to riches, but his reversed destiny was from the palace to the pit, which is a rare and more devastating occurrence.

Of course, he was emotionally devastated, socially ostracized, physically disabled, and economically impoverished. I personally believe that the statement of the fire of God and his wife pronunciation to curse God and die, were incorporated as a stumbling block to drive a wedge between him and God; intended to cause him to reflect intensively on the righteousness of God, hence questioning Gods integrity—but he was spiritually strong. He exercised childlike humility and humbled himself before the Lord.

Because he had met Christ Jesus in the core of his spirit, and had identified with him, he could say, the Lord giveth and he taketh away, though he slays me, yet will I trust him, though my flesh might be destroyed yet with my eyes I will see God, for I know that my redeemer lives and I will stand with him on that day. He was at that place in God that every believer should endeavor to reach. He pressed towards the mark for the prize of the high calling through trials and tribulation and in the end, God was glorified.

...

Abraham went with Isaac his son to make of him a sacrifice unto God. This was the promised seed, the son of his old age. Can you imagine the thoughts that might have bombarded his cranium? Can you see him lagging the pace of this journey? Can you see him asking God why, in his mind? Or, maybe because of his prior knowledge of God he was willing to make any sacrifice without flinching. Who knows, the mountain probably seemed steeper than normal that day. The task was great, his emotions must have been challenged, but his attitude of steadfastness is worth emulating. His love for God, and his humility to the cause, surpasses selfishness. He knew that the God whom he served was able to raise up his son from the dead. As a result, his faith and belief in God were accounted unto him for righteousness, and he became a friend of God. Abraham had no knowledge that God was testing him. He was simply pressing towards the mark for the prize of the high calling through trials and tribulation that God might be glorified.

...

David met the Lord and learned humility, behaved himself wisely, learned to forgive, have compassion and to be just. When Goliath appeared in his life to exalt himself against the God of the

Israelites, he did not look at the tremendous sight, neither size of the enemy, but he asked about the prize. He could draw from his experiences of slaying a lion and a bear, and execute accordingly, in a most befitting manner, considering Goliath less than the lion and the bear that he had defeated. Though David had a somewhat rollercoaster lifestyle, in the end, he earned the title of being a man after God's own heart. Here we see where quality time spent with Christ increases the anointing. Regardless of his trials and temptations he pressed towards the mark for the prize of the high calling and God was glorified.

...

Daniel was cast into the lion's den. Shadrach, Meshach, and Abednego were cast into the fiery furnace, but their testimony was that even if God didn't choose to deliver, 'we will not bow'. Fear must have come, doubt must have appeared, but perfect love casts it all out.

The believer is then required to continually press towards the mark for the prize of the high calling in Christ Jesus through fasting, prayer, and holy living. The believer is required to know God and develop a relationship with him through his words.

The believer is expected to identify with Christ through his name, and by his spirit. He or she is expected to tell of Christ in the flesh, but more importantly, be renewed in the spirit of his or her mind.

Finally, the believer should not be conformed to the system of human thoughts and behavior, as he or she is expected to walk by faith and not by sight, having the attitude of humility as his or her guide.

From the day the believer accepted Jesus Christ as his or her personal Savior, baptized in his name, got filled with his Holy Spirit, that believer has entered warfare. Whether it is upon the believer's marriage, children, business, or on the job, the believer is in a war. It is a war for the soul. It does not matter how subtle it seems.

Every spirit of distraction and marginal bands, every avenue used to cause doubt or insecurity and fear are indeed weapons to incapacitate, breakdown and impair the vision and purpose to the believer's God given rights.

The devils know what heaven is like, and their duty is to stop the believer from getting there. The believer is therefore encouraged to study to show him and herself approved unto God—holding on to the unchanging hands of the Lord.

In that regard, the believer is encouraged to be steadfast, unmovable, always abounding in the work of the Lord, forasmuch as he or she knows that his and her labor is not in vain in the Lord (1Cor.15: 58).

Chapter Ten
A Higher Place of Praise

I firmly believe that though we were born with a nature that attracts sin, we were also born with a vacuum within that yearns for fellowship with God. In that regard, I believe that every believer can live a victorious life, in spite of past mistakes and the inevitable war of circumstances. I believe the great men and women of old had issues in their secular lives, grave ordeals, and unexpected circumstances to put up with—but they still made it to the heavenly halls of fame.

The same Paul who says that there is a war in his members, so much so, that the good things that he would do, he finds himself not doing, and the evil things that he would not do, he finds himself doing, is the same Paul that said, he had fought a good fight, kept the faith, and finished his course.

What then did these men know that we don't? What did they do? What are their secrets, if any, and why did the Lord favor them? Men like Adam, Enoch, Abraham, Noah, Moses, Joshua, Elijah, David, and John the Revelator to name a few.

To critically analyze these men, one must first study their patterns of life, group them accordingly and see what they had in common, then highlight their high and low points and examine their behaviors in these different circumstances. Nevertheless, the question remains: what did these guys do to reach the mark for the prize of the high calling in God?

Was it by works of righteousness? Was it by class, royalty, status or heritage? Or was it their academics, in terms of eloquence and knowledge? I think not, because Moses even though educated in Egypt, told God that he could not speak (Exodus 4:10).

John, who was one of Jesus' apostles, was a fisherman who was perceived to be unlearned (Acts 4:13).

At the same time, if we travel through the dispensations of time we see where God raised up these great men to deliver his people. Yes, they had opposition, for Janess and Jambress opposed Moses, Jezebel challenged Elijah, Saul battled with David, John was thrown into the Isle of Patmos.

Yes, they had weaknesses and faults, for David slept with Bathsheba, Uriah's wife. Moses struck the rock twice when he should have spoken to it, (2 Sam. 11, Num. 20:7-11).

And, of course they had apprehensions as ordinary men do, because fear overtook Elijah, and he ran from Jezebel when she threatens to take his head off; incidentally, that was right after he successfully executed four hundred and fifty false prophets that she endorsed (1kings 19).

Even Abraham, the father of faith, had insecurities. He went down into Egypt because of a famine and had to lie that his wife was his sister; more surprisingly, he slept with Hagar, his wife's handmaid, to fulfill the promise of God, instead of waiting on the Lord to have a son with his wife (Gen. 12:10-20, 16:4-8).

Every one of these men were flawed; therefore, this commentary is not, in any way, endorsing sin, it is simply saying that there is no condemnation to them that are in Christ Jesus, who walk not after the flesh, but after the Spirit (Rom. 8:1).

Therefore, instead of asking what did these guys do to reach the mark for the prize of the high calling, the question then should be: what did God see in them that earned them a place in the heavenly halls of fame?

Let's examine it. With Adam, God came down in the cool of the day into the Garden of Eden and spent quality time with him—well, we know he was innocent.

Enoch walked with God three hundred years after he begat Methuselah, and he was not, for God took him (Gen.5v24). The testimony of Enoch was that he pleased God; therefore, that means he had faith—for without faith, it is impossible to please God.

With Abraham, on one occasion, God said, "shall I hide from

Abraham that thing which I do, seeing that Abraham shall surely become a great and mighty nation, and all the nations of the earth shall be blessed in him?" (Gen.18v17-18). It is then deduced that Abraham was a friend of God—for only your friends know your deepest secrets.

As for Noah the scriptures records, "But Noah found grace in the eyes of the Lord. Noah was a just man and perfect in his generation, and Noah walked with God" (Gen. 6:8-9).

Most intriguingly, Moses spoke to God face to face and had frequent dialogues (Exod. 33:11).

When we examine the above testimonies and scriptures, it is consistent where these patriarchs had a one-on-one relationship with God. It is also evident that they all had a strong desire to please God.

However, I found out that the major and most important thing that these men had in common and the thing that led them to the hall of fame in the scriptures, was that same thing which allowed them to reach the higher calling in Jesus Christ.

It was the same thing that led them to know God, and it was the one thing that God looked at. The very thing which separated them from their brethren and fellow men. Oh yes, the same thing that we all need to get there—was their hearts.

Why the heart?

Simply because it is the mirror of the inner man; it's a reflection of whatever is demonstrated in words and deeds. The Bible said that a good man out of the good treasure of his heart bringeth forth that which is good, and an evil man out of the evil treasure of his heart bringeth forth that which is evil, for of the abundance of the heart his mouth speaks (Luke. 6:45).

In the book of Psalms, the question is asked and answered. It says, 'Who shall ascend into the hill of the Lord? Or who shall stand in his holy place? He that hath clean hands and a pure heart' (Psalm 24:3-4).

...

When God had sent Samuel to anoint one of Jesse's sons to be king over Israel the scripture says: 'And it came to pass when they were come, that he looked on Eliab, and said, surely the Lord's anointed is before him. But the Lord said unto Samuel, look not on his countenance or on the height of his stature, because I have refused him: for the Lord sees not as man see for man looks on the outward appearance, but the Lord looks on the heart' (1Sam.16: 6-7).

And if you remember clearly, God had to give king Saul a new heart to govern his people.

David as a result could say to his son, Solomon after him, 'And thou Solomon my son, know thou the God of thy father, and serve him with a perfect heart and with a willing mind, for the Lord searches all hearts, and understands all the imaginations of the thoughts: if thou seek him he will be found of thee, but if thou forsake him, he will cast thee off for ever' (1Chron. 28:9).

Again, David records, 'Search me, O God, and know my heart, try me and know my thoughts: and see if there be any wicked way in me, and lead me in the way everlasting' (Psalm 139:23).

Solomon found it out later and records in Proverbs that, 'Every way of a man is right in his own eyes, but the Lord ponders the hearts' (Prov. 21:2).

God says, 'I the Lord search the heart, I try the reins, even to give every man according to his ways, and according to the fruits of his doings' (Jer.17:10).

Why the heart? Simply because out of the heart proceeds the issues of life. So, by this we see where the heart condition plays a vital role in success of the life of a believer.

When I speak of the heart in this context, I am speaking of the conscience, attitude, behavior, moral and ethics and all the attributes that are summed up in the word love.

This heart of love is the source that hinges all resources. It's like the axis on which the universe spins. It is the medium of revelation, the act of creation; it's the fulfillment of all commandments. It is the power of God. This love is patient, longsuffering, kind, diligent, compassionate, and true.

It is not puffed up, as stated in the book of Corinthians. It seeks not its own but looks out for the wealth and welfare of others and rejoices therewith. This love is not a goodwill sort of love, or a charitable metaphor that is used by the impressionists, the eye servants, or the men pleasers; instead, it is devoted to the cause and the will of God.

When one has this kind of love, and the relationship with God is intact, then this heart of love is the greatest weapon in any warfare. This is the love that covers a multitude of sins and brought Jesus into the world to die for the sins of men. This is the love that he had that while he was on the cross you and I were on his mind; he could say father forgive them. This love embodies the fruit of the spirit—and against such, there is no law.

The love that will make us lay down our lives for the brethren. This love desires the justice and righteousness of God. This is not the Philia love, nor the Eros love. This is the Agape love.

This love brings about focus, it brings direction, and it is unconditional. It differentiates the temporal from spiritual; it makes it easy to forgive. It sets things in order of priority; it sees less of self and more of people. It makes a person wish that none should perish but that all would have eternal life; it sees through the eyes of God.

This was the heart that Stephen had, while he was stoned, he could look into heaven and see Jesus, and in the end, he could say, 'Lord, lay not this sin to their charge' (Acts 7:54 - 60).

The love I am talking about is the love that will make a person love his or her enemy and do good to them that despitefully use and say all manner of evil against him or her, for Jesus' sake.

A heart without this kind of love can never handle power. This was the love that Moses had, for when God was about to kill the Israelites in the wilderness because of their provocation unto the Lord, Moses could plead on their behalf (Numbers 14:11-20).

David possessed this kind of love for God and his fellowmen. In his zeal he could say, 'What shall be done to the man that kill this Philistine, and taketh away the reproach from Israel? For who is this uncircumcised Philistine, that he should defy the armies of the living God' (1 Sam. 17:26).

Regardless of the mishaps that would befall David in his later years, his devotion to God and his fellowmen was unprecedented; he was later known as a man after God's own heart.

This is the ingredient of the stalwarts of old. As Moses said to the Lord, 'I beseech thee show me thy glory' and he said, 'I will make all my goodness pass before thee, and I will proclaim the name of the Lord before thee, and will be gracious to whom I will be gracious, and will shew mercy to whom I will show mercy; and he said thou canst not see my face for there shall no man see me, and live.' And the Lord said, "Behold there is a place by me and thou shalt stand upon a rock and it shall come to pass while my glory passes by, that I will put thee in a cleft of the rock and will cover thee with my hand while I pass by: and I will take away mine hand and thou shalt see my back parts but my face shall not be seen' (Exodus 33:18-23).

This is the place every believer should endeavor to reach, but first the heart must be purged then one must stand on the rock and that rock is Jesus Christ.

Therefore, a person does not need to repeat lines of affirmations and use omens as the sorcerers do. One does not need a crystal ball like the witches have. A person does not even need to die in condemnation or self-pity because of the past or present mishaps. Jesus knew that mankind is susceptible to flaws and that's the reason for Calvary. He died that we might have life and that more abundantly. But shall we continue in sin that grace may abound? God forbid! As said before, this is not a license to sin, it is the knowledge that if a person falls, that person should not stay there and die in that position, he or she should pick up him or herself and fight.

Regardless of the closet things that paint pictures of hindrance, if the believer can garner enough courage to confess his or her faults one to the other, if he or she can get the heart right with God; and as much as it is in the believer's power, if he or she can be at peace with his or her fellowmen, then the best is yet to come.

'Wherefore, seeing we also are compassed about with so great a cloud of witnesses, let us lay aside every weight, and the sin which doth so easily beset us, and let us run with patience the race that is set before us, looking unto Jesus the author and finisher of our faith; who for the joy that was set before him endured the cross, despising the shame and is set down at the right hand of the throne of God' (Hebrews12: 1-2).

Chapter Eleven
The Anointed Believer

Pressing towards the mark reflects on finding oneself and the benefits of enduring tribulations. A higher place of praise dealt with the heart condition, and the anointed believer is geared towards showing the believer the criteria of becoming more effective and efficient in ministry.

In that regard, the characteristics that develop anointed believers are enveloped in the following three distinct categories: the daily laws that governs their lifestyle, the priestly worship that they sustain, and the pathway that they traverse.

Though these characteristics chart their lifestyle, it is important to note that they live practical everyday lives. There are no magic formulas, waving of wands, or repeating of words of affirmation to receive the different levels of anointing. The process of receiving the anointing commences and is executed through a set of biblical laws and or righteous principles that are available to whomsoever will access and abide by them. These principles, or laws, react whenever they are tapped into and are activated. And, when they are activated, the responsible agent is able to impact both the spiritual and the natural realm.

In the same manner that the law of aerodynamics keeps a plane in the air, the law or principle of gravity keep objects on the ground, and the law of floatation keep vessels on the water, every natural, spiritual, and psychological aspect, issue, and tendency, is as a result of a set of principles or laws that have been engaged and activated.

Whether for good, or for evil, nothing happens by chance; there is a system of laws that governs the spiritual and the natural world. These laws are built-in, set from the foundation of the world. More importantly, spirits oversee every principle or law that exists. Additionally, these laws are in operation every waking hour of our lives.

If you are old enough to understand, your experience would have already taught you that whatsoever a man sows, that shall he also reap. This is a biblical principle or law that is as old as dirt—set from the foundation of the world and cannot be changed. My grandmother—God bless her soul—used to tell me that I cannot plant corn and expect to reap peas. In that regard, she was telling me to mind my actions, because I was free to choose, but was not free from the consequences of my choices. In other words, I would inevitably reap a field of corn from the seed that I sowed—figuratively of course.

Another law or principle the anointed believers embrace is that of giving. Here, the principle to receive, is to give. Giving of time, giving of substance, giving of resources, becoming selfless, opening the bowels of compassion, extending empathy. Not to hoard or withhold, but to release—meaning, not to hold back, but to let go. It is much like sowing what is expected to be reaped. This is not about being slack or free handed, not through coercion or manipulation, it is not about being simple, gullible, or naïve, falling for whims and scams. It is about stewardship; it is about hearing from God, following his instructions, and responsibly responding to his service or the needs of his people.

This principle might be mesmerizing to many because it defies the wisdom of the world, but in this regard, God chooses the foolish things of the world to confound the wise.

The skeptic should realize that everything belongs to God. The scripture states that the earth is the Lord's. And, it is God who gives power to gain wealth. Therefore, when a person understands and gives responsibly for a righteous cause, that person open doors of understanding, intuition, access, and favor into his or her own life.

Nevertheless, in giving to receive, the spirit behind the giving must be immersed in the attitude of giving cheerfully without the fanfare—that is, discreetly, outside of the limelight, and with good intentions. The scripture says, God loves a cheerful giver; but more importantly, he who gives to the poor, lends to God, and God is no debtor to man; that means, he will repay—and when God gives or repays, he gives good measure, pressed down, shaken together, and running over.

Another principle or law that governs the lifestyle of the anointed believer is conveyed through a soft answer that turns away wrath. Think about an arrogant person hurling accusation and condemnation at an innocent individual, and the persecuted individual, instead defending him or herself, or fighting fire with fire, the person responds with a polite, empathetic, non-judgmental answer. The spirit that comes with that soft answer is the spirit of meekness—the reward is that the meek shall inherit the earth (Matt. 5:5).

The contrary vice to a soft answer that turns away wrath is that grievous words stir up anger. Grievous words in this quotation travel with the spirit of anger. To that end, Solomon says, anger rests in the bosom of fools. People who are constantly angry usually have complex underlying issues.

I strongly believe, and a matter of fact, it has been proven that through the temperament and the spirit of a person, certain ailments can be diagnosed. For example, when a person worries and stresses him or herself, the immune system is compromised; at such time, some women complain of hormone imbalance in these instances of stress. Some doctors now conclude that through stress, the arteriole walls develop plaque, and as a result, the blood pressure increases. Hence, these people usually suffer from hypertension.

However, not all of these are a result of anger, some of these ailments are hereditary, some are the effect of deficiency diseases, others are because of sin, and some for God to be glorified (John 9:1-4).

A few proverbial speeches that are directly attached to a set of principles or laws are as follows: righteousness exalts a nation, but sin is a reproach unto any people; honor thy father and they mother, that thy days may be long upon the land; whatsoever a man sows, that he also shall reap; he that sows in tears, shall reap in joy; whatsoever is done in darkness will come out in the light; with the measure that you mete, it will be meted unto you; he that loves his life shall lose it, but he that lose his life for Christ's sake shall find it; it is not what goes into the mouth that defiles, but that which comes out of the mouth; death and life are in the power of the tongue; if two of you shall agree on earth as touching anything that they shall ask, it shall be done for them of my father; ask and it shall be given, seek and ye shall find, knock and it shall be opened unto you; and, cast your bread upon the waters for you shall find it after many days.

Pages would not be enough to list and explain life lessons, beatitudes, laws, and commandments that contain the principles that governs the daily lifestyle of the anointed believer. However, listed above are a few of the countless proverbial speeches and deeds that contain the laws and principles that govern the issues, tendencies, and spirituality of human beings. These laws and principles are embedded in human nature and can be elicited from every human interaction. And, understanding, and embracing or refraining from them, are expected to be gracious and spontaneous; but sadly, because of iniquity, the loving hearts of men are wax cold—therefore, the positive laws and principles have become hard to observe.

In this regard, for the believer to abide in the anointing, he or she must intentionally train the mind to appreciate these laws and principles and react to them graciously, spontaneously, and appropriately.

Apostle Paul spoke of these principles and laws when he mentioned that there is a law or war among his members. A tug to do evil instead of good, he also spoke about lawful things that were not expedient and that he would not be brought under that law. Hence, as believers, one has to regulate what is transmitted through the spiritual realm to one's benefit; in that, the believer must control and then guard his or her actions and speech with diligence to maneuver these principles and laws. The scripture warns that: 'he that hath no rule over his own spirit is like a city that is broken down and without walls' (Prov. 25:28).

It is interesting to note that the devils will be satisfied if the believer is a simple church going person. Wishy washy. Lukewarm.

The devils would not mind if the believer does not guard the doors of his or her lips and does not allow God to order his or her steps. The devils would be happy if the believer accepts life in whatsoever form, it presents itself.

The devils would be most comfortable if the believer speaks against his or her own prosperity, because of temporary setbacks, inability, or moments of lack. If the devils can get the believer to block his or her own blessings, by way of his or her own speech, their work is done. The devils know that whatsoever the believer binds on earth is bound in heaven—they know too, that whatsoever the believer does in the spiritual realm, through prayer, will inevitably impact the natural realm. More importantly, they know that, like God's words, the believer's words are spirit, and they are life—and they will accomplish whatsoever they are set out to do (Isa. 55:11, Jn. 6:63).

In this light, the acts the believer sometimes commit, and the things that he or she idly says and does, might appear to be trivial, but those mindless and sinful deeds, whether actions or speech, create ditches and craters in the spiritual realm and cause a chain reaction of repercussions in the natural realm.

Sometimes the believer feels as though he or she is powerless against the loose speeches and so, to satisfy the conscience, in order to achieve a false peace, the believer repeat babbles such as: God is not through with me yet. I am taking time to transform to Christian living. I was already expose. It's in my nature. I am not guilty of the very bad ones. God understands. I am only human.

The comforting part to this dilemma is that God winks at the believer in times of ignorance (Acts. 17:30). Nevertheless, in that same scripture, he commands the believer to repent. That's because there are two sides to these equations—the wages of sin is death, but the gift of God is eternal life. Righteousness exalts a nation, but sin is a reproach to any people.

Every dead work of the flesh is just as bad as the other and whether it is done a little, or much, it is of the same detriment. In fact, dead works are seeds planted, that inevitably will germinate and produce in abundance and open doors in the spirit and give entrance to demons and rights to the devil over the believer.

These set principles are not only tapped into when one speak and do the actions, if the very thoughts dwell upon sin, that sin will begin to permeate the spirit and eventually the believer's presence until it overwhelms him or her. One writer says, as a man thinks, so is he.

Therefore, since the responsibility of every believer is to fulfill his/her God given purposes and to operate in his/her calling, it is imperative and advisable that the believer observe the set principles that will attract the anointing and propels him or her to higher heights and deeper depths in Christ. The anointed believers are accustomed to these rules, and they observe them.

...

In addition to the righteous principles and laws that governs the life of the anointed believer, he or she must sustain an environment that lends itself to priestly worship. In this position, the anointed believer is a priest first to God, then to his or her family, then to whatever pocket of the vineyard that God places or appoints him or her, whether it is the community, the town, or the nation—in this regard, the anointed believer is an ambassador of Christ.

Let us examine a few natural and supernatural historical biblical events to establish the platform of priestly worship that the anointed believer is appointed to and is required to sustain.

In the book of the prophet Ezekiel, God showed the first state of Lucifer when he created him. The scripture said, 'Thou hast been in Eden the garden of God, every precious stone was thy covering, the Sardius, Topaz and the Diamond, the Beryl, the Onyx and the Jasper, the Sapphire, the Emerald, and the Carbuncle, and Gold: the workmanship of thy tabrets and of thy pipes was prepared in thee in the day that thou wast created. Thou art the anointed cherub that covereth and I have set thee so: thou wast upon the holy mountain of God; thou hast walked up and down in the midst of the stones of fire. Thou wast perfect in thy ways from the day that thou wast created, till iniquity was found in thee' (Ezekiel 28:13-15).

This scripture gave us a detailed description of Lucifer's adornment, his appointment, and his dwelling place at that time. Every precious stone was his covering, he was the anointed cherub, and he was in Eden, the garden of God.

Let's start this study with the precious stones. Historically, rulers adorn themselves with precious stones symbolically for the purpose it represents—whether it is to show authority, legitimacy, victory, or even tradition. For example, kings wear crowns and signet rings as a symbol of legitimacy and authority.

Lucifer, being the anointed cherub, and being in Eden, the garden of God, suggested that he was a high-ranking angel with high authority and legitimacy as represented by the stones he wore in his garment as presented in the quotation above. Along with his high authority, he had dominion over God's creation and influence over angels—until iniquity was found in him and he was cast out of heaven (Isa. 14:12-15, Rev. 12).

Let's equate Adam's authority to that of Lucifer, using a similar perspective. Adam was created in the image and likeness of God—which means, he was sinless and holy, possessing wisdom, and a heart of pure love. God then placed Adam in Eden, and gave him dominion, authority, and power, to subdue everything in the earth, the air above, and the sea (Gen. 1:26-28, Ps. 8:4-8).

Nevertheless, when Adam sinned, he lost his innocent adornment, his appointment, and his dwelling place.

The scripture then says, 'just as sin came into the world through one man, and death through sin, and so death spreads to all men because all sinned.'

Here, it can be said that everyone became guilty of sin and would experience death, since everyone was in the loins of Adam. In other words, if Adam's original sin cause everyone to be born in sin and shaped in iniquity, it simple means Adam had authority over the destiny of humanity.

Therefore, it is safe to say that every nation was in Adam's loins and as a result, he had dominion and authority over mankind even before they came into existence. Nevertheless, though he never wore the stones as Lucifer did, the precious stones were present in the garden with him. Only, he never needed to wear them—truth be told, he was in a state of innocence, naked (Gen 2: 12, 3:9-10).

Let us shift gears from Lucifer and Adam for a moment and examine a more intrinsic factor that will take us closer to the essence of this study on priestly worship that the anointed believer should sustain.

God gave special and specific instructions to Moses on how

to design and make Aaron's garments. The scripture states the following: 'And thou shalt speak unto all that are wise hearted whom I have filled with the spirit of wisdom, that they may make Aaron's garments to consecrate him that he may minister unto me in the priest's office...And thou shalt set in it settings of stones, even four rows of stones: the first row shall be a Sardis, a Topaz and a Carbuncle: this shall be the first row. And the second row shall be an Emerald, a Sapphire and a Diamond. And the third row a Ligure, an Agate and an Amethyst. And the fourth row a Beryl and an Onyx and Jasper: they shall be set in Gold in their inclosing. And the stones shall be with the names of the children of Israel, twelve, according to their names' (Ex.28:1-21).

If you look carefully at the parallel in terms of the covering and garments, you will notice that the precious stones that were woven in the composition of Lucifer's covering before he was stripped and kicked out of heaven, are the same types of precious stones that were etched in the breastplate of the garment that God gave instructions to Moses to create and consecrate for Aaron.

And, as we already declared, the stones authenticated legitimacy, represented authority, and signifies power. That divine responsibility was now endowed upon Aaron as a priest of God. Aaron was now privileged with governmental authority and responsibility to go before God on behalf of the nation of Israel. The garment was etched with the inscription: Holiness unto the Lord (Ex.28: 36). He had the anointing because of his appointment and his consecration (Ex.28: 41).

He was covered with precious stones and wore the garments of righteousness and ministered unto God in the Holy of Holies, or in his Eden.

Like Lucifer and Adam before him, he had at his disposal, the adornment, the appointment, and the dwelling place.

Lucifer was there but was cast out, Adam was also there, and he transgressed; hence, he was cast out of Eden, and a Cherub was placed at the entrance to stop him from getting back.

To reiterate, in Aaron's time, God decided to do a new thing. He duplicated a replica of Eden upon the land. He created it in the form of the Holy of Holies of the tabernacle, and Aaron was now placed in that most exalted position in which, once per year, he was responsible to go before God on behalf of the nation of Israel.

What then is the meaning of this study with precious stones? Let's go a little further; John the revelator in the Isle that is called Patmos had a vision of the New Jerusalem. The scripture states that, '...and I saw a new heaven and a new earth; for the first heaven and the first earth were passed away; and there was no more sea. And I John saw the holy city, new Jerusalem coming down from God out of heaven, prepared as a bride adorned for her husband, and I heard a great voice out of heaven saying, behold, the tabernacle of God is with men' (Rev.21:1-3).

'And the foundation of the walls of the city were garnished with all manner of precious stones. The first foundation was Jasper; the second Sapphire; the third Chalcedony; the fourth an Emerald; the fifth Sardonyx: the sixth Sardis; the seventh Chrysolite; the eighth Beryl; the ninth a Topaz; the tenth a Chrysoprasus; the eleventh a Jacinth; the twevelth an Amethyst' (Rev.21:19-20).

Here, the New Jerusalem that John saw, was adorned with the same precious stones that freckled the landscape of the Garden of Eden; the same precious stones that once covered Lucifer; the same precious stones that were etched in the breastplate of the garment of the priest who represented the children of Israel when he made appearances in the Holy of Holies.

In essence, the New Jerusalem is prepared for heirs to the kingdom. Holy men. Anointed men. Men whose motto is Holiness unto the Lord. Men who understand priestly worship and live thereby. Men whose garments are spotless and washed in the blood of the lamb. Men who are overcomers—that is, the believer.

Again, Lucifer had governmental authority, he was in the garden of God but got kicked out. Adam was in government and had similar authority; he too was in the garden of God. He had dominion over the earth and ruled everything that was in it, but he transgressed.

Now we see Aaron wearing the stones on his breastplate, attached to his shoulder as a yoke. That meant, governmental authority was yoke upon his shoulder. He was there authorized to go before God on behalf of the nation of Israel.

Nevertheless, in the days of Aaron, only the High Priest could enter the Holy place. Only the High Priest could wear the stones

The Christian Soldier 145

and stand before God, and so God had to change that so that every person can have the chance to become a priest.

In that regard, it is not the will of God that any man should perish, but sin must be punished; therefore, God made Jesus to take on the sin that everyone committed and punish him on the cross for everyone. The scripture says, 'For he made him who knew no sin to be sin for us, that we might become the righteous of God in him (2 Corr.5:21).

The scriptures went on further to say, 'Therefore, as through one man's offense judgment came to all men, resulting in condemnation, even so through one man's righteous act the free gift came to all men, resulting in justification of life (Romans 5:18). This action of Jesus satisfied the sin debt of Adam, redeemed humanity, and opened doors so that whosoever desire can experience the righteousness of God.

This is where it becomes interesting. The prophet Isaiah prophesied of Jesus Christ by saying: 'For unto us a child is born, unto us a son is given: and the government shall_be upon his shoulder: and his name shall be called Wonderful, Councilor, The Mighty God, The Everlasting Father, The Prince of peace.' (Isaiah 9:6).

In this position came Jesus, with the government on his shoulders, "the stones upon his shoulder." Having dominion over everything, having all power and authority, having all glory and majesty. He, being far above thrones, dominions, principalities and powers, came down in the form of flesh to pay the price of sin with his life at Calvary to redeem the world through his blood.

As a result, he became the High Priest of our salvation. What am I saying? I am saying that Jesus Christ won back everything from Lucifer and now stands as the mediator between God and man. Having governmental authority over the entire human race.

However, Jesus did not leave it there, he yoked himself with the believers that the believers through his redeeming blood can partake in his presence, grace, and power.

In that regard, the scripture states that, 'Beloved, now are we the sons of God, and it doth not yet appear what we shall be: but we know that when he shall appear we shall be like him, for we shall see him as he is' (1 John 3:2).

Another writer puts it this way, 'And if children, then heirs, heirs of God and joint heirs with Christ; if so be that we suffer with him, that we may be also glorified together' (Romans 9:17).

But most rewardingly, to grip the case in point, the scriptures state clearly that: 'we are a chosen generation, a royal priesthood, an holy nation, a peculiar people; that ye should show forth the praises of him who hath called you out of darkness into his marvelous light' (1 Peter 2:9). Here, in this scripture the privilege of being a part of the royal priesthood has been conferred on the believer—this is done through the transforming power of Jesus Christ.

In addition to the quote above, the scripture also states that, 'Unto him that loved us and washed us from our sins in his own blood, and hath made us kings and priests unto God and his Father, to him be glory and dominion for ever and ever amen' (Rev. 1:5-6).

Lucifer had the anointing before he fell. Adam had it before he was locked out of Eden, and Aaron basked in it as a priest of God. In like manner, God made the believers kings and priests and gave them power. The scripture says, 'But ye shall receive power, after that the Holy Ghost is come upon you: and ye shall be witnesses unto me both in Jerusalem, and in all Judea, and in Samaria, and unto the uttermost part of the earth' (Acts 1:8).

And, 'Verily, verily, I say unto you, he that believeth on me, the works that I do shall he do also; and greater works than these shall he do because I go unto my father' (John 14:12).

Therefore, the anointed believer, is in the position of the priests, because God placed him or her there. The anointed believers could not go to Eden, so Christ brought Eden to them when they received the Holy Spirit. As a result, the anointed believer has the adornment, the appointment, and is in dwelling place.

In that regard, the anointed believers are little pieces of heaven on earth. They are in a position of governmental authority; they are in a place of dominion and power—they are precious gems in God's sight. They are the ambassadors of Christ. They have the power to bind and to loose. And, whatever they bind, or loose, is endorsed, sanctioned, and approved in heaven.

When the devils see them, the devils recognize them from afar and tremble at their speech and presence.

Therefore, believers, have a passion for the stones on your breastplate and shoulders, remembering what they represent.

As mentioned in chapter six with the extended blessing of the armor, the believers are anointed as the priests, hence their concern extends to their family, the neighbor, the brethren, community, the city or the state that God appoints and assign them.

In that regard, the anointed believer should sustain an environment conducive to priestly worship, an environment that is free from idle speech and loose livelihood.

He or she must take charge of the principles and laws that govern the world and use them to his or her advantage. The believers must sustain an environment of worship, knowing that they are in the King of kings' domain; and that their names are among the spiritual hierarchy of the land; therefore, they must practice kingdom principles, kingdom speech, kingdom power, kingdom anointing, and kingdom lifestyle.

The anointed believers are in government. As a result, their motto must be, Holiness unto The Lord!

If the believer is already operating on this plain, then he or she is able to speak to affairs of concern—even in the political arena— that determine decisions.

Let the voices of the anointed be heard.

The believers are expected to practice kingdom principles, speaking to every attitude, intent, purpose, and vision, bringing the entire body, mind, and spirit under subjection into the will of God. The believers are expected to be constantly alert, having the awareness that they are ambassadors of Christ.

The believers are expected to practice kingdom speech, having their speech seasoned with salt that it may administer grace unto the ears of the listener. Letting the word of God dwell richly in their spirit, refraining from idle words and lewd speeches, which are a breach in the spirit. Speaking positively through faith, calling into their lives and the lives of others, the things that are lacking, and seeing it come to pass.

Speaking as a representative of God. Speaking as one on the board of directors, speaking as a person in government, as the priest, the joint heir, speaking as one having permission from the King, to execute at will, the judgment necessary.

The cloud of witnesses of anointed believers are all over the scriptures. They had power to move mountains, they had authority over land, sea, and air, which means that they had dominion in the earth. They prophesied and dictated to the spiritual realm to their benefit: Moses stretched out his rod across the Red Sea and the waters were parted. Elisha hit Jordan River with his mantle and the waters were parted. Peter walked with Jesus on the sea. Elijah called fire from heaven and burned up his enemies twice. He also challenged the false prophets of Baal that his God would answer by fire from heaven, and it happened. Moses said, "who is on the Lord's side, come over here". Those who didn't dare to go to him; the earth rented and swallowed them. Joshua spoke to the sun and the earth's rotation lingered and lengthened the day. Here we see power mixed with faith in action as men took charge over the spiritual realm and establish purpose.

I am through comparing the armed forces and the Kingdom. The little information given on the armed forces is enough to work with. What we need now is to learn how to better arm ourselves against the wiles of the devil and enter into purpose.

Beloved brethren, the principles and patterns of righteousness, and the lives of righteous men, are concisely placed in the scriptures for our benefit. Saints, what was hidden from the wise and prudent is now revealed to babes and suckling.

Therefore, study to show yourselves approved unto God, and in the same breath, remember that they that will live godly must suffer persecution.

The believer should therefore be aware that when washed in the blood of the lamb, sanctified by the spirit, and believe in holiness, attacks will come, and the fight is not so much of a physical battle.

Victory over evil is in the preparation of the temple and the execution of righteous principles. That is what will define the outcome; the rest is for God, for the battle is the Lord's.

In the same manner that God words will not return unto him void but will accomplish that which they are set out to do, the believer's words have similar creative and operational power. For there is no speech or language where their voice is not heard.

God calls the things that are not, as though they were. Hence, the believer can, by faith, speak as God spoke, because the believer is a son of God and joint-heirs with Christ. Therefore, he or she can speak to mountains and be delivered.

The believer has the power and authority to rebuke sicknesses and infirmities and see them dispersed. He or she has the privilege to direct his or her future by way of speaking. The believer has power over all the powers of the enemy—that is, power and dominion over the land, the sea, and the air.

Therefore, maximize your potential in Christ Jesus. Speak to God in prayer as a priest in your land and let the nations be delivered, and the lands healed. Stand in the gap for sinners, pray to God for their souls, speak into the heavenly places and tear down principalities and powers, and rulers of the darkness of this world, and spiritual wickedness in high places.

Identify yourself, know who you are, understand your anointing and your purpose. Operate in your calling, maximize the gifts of the spirit, speak positively and speak blessings to everyone. Motivate, encourage, reassure, for the God of Jacob is your refuge; he will never leave you nor forsake you.

He that hath an ear, let him hear what the spirit saith unto the churches, to him that overcome will I give to eat of the hidden manna, and will give him a white stone and in the stone a new name written which no man knoweth saving he that receiveth it' (Rev 2:17).

...

The path the anointed believer traverse is probably the most demanding of the characteristics that develops the believer's character. It is a path designed for self-denial and total reliance on Jesus. The path is lonely, humbling, demands sacrifice, is of a repetitive nature, and is extremely tedious.

At the same time, the path sharpens the believer's inner ear to distinguish the voice of Jesus amidst a plethora of noise or distractors.

The path develops a steadfast attitude in the believer to become effectual and fervent in prayer; the path develops trust, strengthens belief, and emboldens the faith that calls the things that are not as though they are.

It is a path that defies even the natural senses—it teaches the believer to look beyond what was, what is, and to see the possibilities of what can be.

It is then pertinent that everyone who traverse the path, have a guide or a mentor. Many believers disregard the need for a shepherd when they traverse this path, but a shepherd is needed here more than ever—a shepherd who is a tour guide, and not a travel agent, a shepherd who has been there and is willing to travel along instead of pointing out the destination.

Without a mentor or a guide, the aspiring believer will fight battles and have victories when traveling along this path, but the impact that he or she would have had in the war if he/she was under an umbrella, or understood the paradigm of sons, would have increased exponentially.

Sadly, many are totally unaware of scriptural father-son relationship and the transferring of anointing. Of course, they might have listened to preachers of dynamic prestige and leadership excellence, they might have listened to mighty men of valor, who impacted their lives for a season, but there is something in the aura and essence of humility in sonship that attracts the anointing.

The anointed believer usually has a mentor, or spiritual father that enhances and authenticate his or her ministry. The mentor or spiritual father guides and take the mentee to places he or she has never been in the spiritual realm.

With that said, let us examine a biblical reference of the path the anointed believer takes, in the book of kings. The scripture states that, 'And it came to pass, when the Lord would take up Elijah into heaven by a whirlwind, that Elijah went with Elisha from Gilgal' (2 Kings 2:1).

The picture in this physical yet spiritual journey captured Elijah and Elisha on a path from Gilgal, to Bethel, to Jericho and then to Jordan, consecutively.

Before we delve into patterns of comparisons, let us first look at the place Gilgal and its spiritual significance as it relates to other events.

First, Gilgal is a place located east of Jericho (Jos 4 :19).

The word Gilgal refers to whirlwind, wheel, or the rolling away of the reproach of Egypt, or as in the tearing away of the flesh in circumcision—a regeneration, or washing, renewal, and cleansing

(Jos 5: 9).

Incidentally, Gilgal was the first place that the Israelites camped on their route to the promise land of Canaan after crossing the Jordan river (Jos 4 v 19-20).

It was the place where the Israelites kept the first Passover in the land of Canaan (Jos 5 v 10).

Gilgal is also the place where all Israel went to renew the kingdom and their allegiance to king Saul (1 Sam 11: 14).

Sadly, Gilgal is also referred to as a center of idolatry by the early prophets in their days (Hos 4: 15, 9: 15, 12: 11) and (Amos 4: 4, 5: 5). Hence, the region of Gilgal marks a milestone in the life of Israel.

Elijah went with Elisha from Gilgal and the two went to Bethel. Here, Bethel is referred to as the house of God, the place where the altar is, a place of devotion and dedication, a place of worship and spiritual empowerment (Gen. 28:16-19, 35:1).

The journey then continues to Jericho—this city was referred to as the city of palms because of its abundance of palm trees. It was a fenced city with a secured fortress with high formidable walls, a stronghold. In the land of Canaan, it was the most important city. Yet, it was a massive hurdle, an obstacle, a place which encourages fear and intimidation.

Then the journey continued and ended at Jordan. Jordan means the descender or flowing downwards. Jordan is always overflowing its banks during harvest, it was a place of depth, where billows roar; interestingly, at the mention of Jordan, all the inhabitants of the nearby land became fearful because of the deeds that Jehovah God performed there in defense of the children of Israel (Joshua 3:15; 5:1).

Finally, at the end of the journey, the heavenly hosts appeared; the mentor went away, the mantle fell, and the mentee received the anointing. This is a time of crowning, miracles, blessings, appointments, and increased anointing (2 Kings 2:12-14).

The path of the anointed believer is consistent in the scriptures with the anointed men and women of God. Here Elisha brought Elijah through the route preparing him to become his successor, a prototype with a double anointing. This path illustrates an incubation period between Jordan and Jericho, two extremes with a middle ground offering not only promised glory, but a decline into idolatry.

Every new-born believer has been here. Everyone was born in sin and shaped in iniquity—a type of bondage like that of the Israelites in Egypt. Everyone must cross the desert to the promised land. And, everyone must approach Gilgal.

Gilgal is the beginning.

It is the place where the believer rolls away of the reproach of Egypt, it is the place for the tearing away of the flesh as in circumcision—it is a place for a regeneration, a washing, renewal, and cleansing.

Here, the believer will see the cycle, see the monotonous drag of a lifestyle repeating itself again and again. Here the believer must decide on his or her own whether to stay on this cycle or to go on to the next level.

In essence, Gilgal can be considered that place that offers stagnation, procrastination, a cyclic lackadaisical influence; yet it is the place that prompt the deciding factor that effect change. It is the wall of fame with hanging portraits and memoirs of those who live to tell.

Lastly, Gilgal can be considered an incubation hub that threatens life yet contains the privileges of resurrection and a renewal of the mind.

After the vision is brought into perspective the believer debusses the whirlwind wheels of Gilgal, and the sanctification of tearing away of the flesh and worldly desire is derived, one must enter Bethel, build an altar, and worship.

Bethel is where the believer meets God. This is the place where instructions will be given, and purpose established. This is where the spirit is fine tuned for the battles to come. This is so because there must be a Jericho in the believer's life on the potter's wheel.

The anointed believer knows that there will be misunderstandings and disappointments along the journey. He or she knows that there will be disagreements. The anointed believer knows that there will be dissatisfactions, he or she knows that sometimes everything will not go as planned or intended, at times, the believer will be marginalized or face embargoes—at times, even between mentor and mentee.

It is at this point—when all hell breaks loose—that Jordan will appear. This is done to test the tenacity of loyalty and strength.

However, at the end, ministering spirits will always present themselves to go where the believer commands, and act at the believer's bidding, showing up into every intricacy or matter that affects the believer.

If a believer doesn't choose to walk this walk and go this route, he or she will end up staying across the banks of Jordan—like the sons of the prophets—having a religious mindset as he or she watches in doubt, insecurity, and limitations, as the brave of his or her brethren climb the ladder of the anointed.

Jesus went this route, in the sense that, he went to Jordan and had his Gilgal there, for fulfillment (Matt. 3:13-15). He then went to the wilderness for his Bethel, and had his devotion, dedication and spiritual empowerment forty days and forty nights (Matt. 4:1-2).

His Jericho appeared with its walls great and tall, filled with indignation and lust, wrath and malice (Matt.4: 3-10). Ultimately, the heavenly host appeared and ministered unto him (Matt. 4:11).

Joshua went to Gilgal with the children of Israel (Joshua 5:7-11). He then led them through Jordan (Joshua 5:1). He brought them to Bethel (Joshua 8: 9-30). Then he brought them to Jericho (Joshua 6:1-5). Eventually the heavenly host appeared unto him (Joshua 5:13-15). This path, as illustrated above, is the path of the anointed believer. It is consistent with the anointed men and women of God in the scriptures and is worth replicating. That is to say, the characteristics that develop the anointed believer are wrapped in righteous living or laws that governs their lifestyle, the priestly worship that they sustain, and the pathway that they traverse.

...

Without going any further, it can be clearly seen that the path of the anointed believer is through rigors, mountain tops, and valleys, hunger and pain, rainy days and dark nights, but at the end of their thorny branches lay the rose bud.

Therefore, since the believers are redeemed by the blood of Jesus Christ, every believer can maximize his or her spiritual potential and receive higher levels of anointing.

The apostle Paul says, 'Laying aside the principle of the doctrine of Christ let us go on to perfection'.

This is where man meets perfection. It is commonly taught that mankind cannot be perfect and live on this earth, but the scripture states otherwise; for example, Noah was a just man and perfect in his generation... (Gen.6: 9). The book of Job refers to Job as a perfect man in the very first verse of the book, and again in verse 8 the God of heaven refers to him as perfect (Job 1:1-8)

In the book of Genesis, it is seen where God told Abraham to walk before him and be perfect (Gen.17: 1).

The same sentiments were echoed by apostle Paul in the book of Corinthians when he said, 'finally brethren, farewell, be perfect, be of good comfort, be of one mind, live in peace, and the God of love and peace shall be with you (2 Cor.13: 11).

And, we cannot overemphasize that God gave the five-fold ministry for the perfecting of the saints (Eph.4:11-12).

But more importantly, the scriptures mention in Psalms that, 'Mark the perfect man and behold the upright, for the end of that man is peace' (Psalm 37:37).

And, I will end on the quote that, 'For in many things, we offend all; if any man offends not in word, the same is a perfect man and is able to bridle the whole body (James. 3:2).

These scriptures tell us that righteousness and the ability to bridle the tongue leads to perfection. Not the absence of faults. Might I add that as long as we are on earth, we will always have faults, but faults in character does not hinder perfection; the inability to live uprightly and to bridle the tongue is what hinders perfection.

Men will always have faults. Faults will take men to the grave—the reason, I believe, why Christ will present us faultless before the presence of his throne (Jude 1:24).

Therefore, it is clearly seen where one can achieve perfection. Perfection does not mean sinless—we are born in sin and shaped in iniquity—the reason why Christ had to die for us, but that's for another conversation. The argument here is that the believers are not perfected to die, they are perfected for ministry—perfection then, is to be whole.

Now it is in this perfection that these principles can be controlled, purpose is established, and the path defined. Therefore, saints of God, whatever the circumstances, do not abort or relent when times become difficult—the only thing that will last is salvation.

Stay consistent and resolute.

Persevere and bring forth that which God is developing in your spirit. Your miracle lies within the path of righteousness. Your change is in your hands. Your test will determine your testimony. Keep in mind that tribulation develops patience, and they that sow in tears shall reap in joy.

The devil intended everything for evil, but God will have it for good. On your journey, keep in mind that diamonds are made by pressure; gold is tried by fire, and pictures are developed in darkness—so is the anointed believer.

Be encouraged in the Lord. On your journey, remember that weeping may endure for a night, but joy comes in the morning. Therefore, reach out for the stone that he that overcome receives, for there is a new name written in it: a new nature, a new anointing.

Now my dear friends, when you have traveled the path and attained into heavenly places through the control of principles and the establishment of purpose, and you begin to speak, and things happen, and you are able to say Lord, and he in return says, here am I—please, let humility be your guide. Allow God to get all the glory. Cast your crown before him in the manner that the four and twenty elders did in the book of revelation (Rev: 4 v10-11).

Do not be misled like the kings of Revelation who will gave up their authority and power (stones) to the Antichrist (Rev: 17v 12-14). Remain faithful to the God of heaven as a true steward. Stay connected to Christ. Beloved...press towards the mark for the prize of the high calling of God in Christ—and remember, the more you sweat in training, the less you bleed in war.

Wherefore seeing we also are compassed about with so great a cloud of witnesses, let us lay aside every weight, and the sin which doth so easily beset us, and let us run with patience the race that is set before us, looking unto Jesus the author and finisher of our faith

Hebrews 12: 1-2

from "Philosophies of The Heart"

New Beginnings
Let's meet, greet, hold hands, walk in the street
Let us hoist our sails like Agamemnon's fleet
And participate in little deeds, not great,
Let us show love and make effort to communicate.
In the end, let us smile and rest for awhile
And show gratitude that once seemed futile

Hush, though time is short, let us not rush,
There's much to feel, see, hear, taste, and touch
Let us spend some time, for little is much. For once,
Let's pamper ourselves and enjoy the ambience.
Life is a treat, there will be no repeat
So, listen to its music and rock to its beat

Reach for its fragrance and capture the aroma,
Inhale the atmosphere and view the panorama
Enjoy the taste and let it linger
Though it might be sweet or sour, salty or bitter
Regard its challenges, and face its opposition
But take time out for romance and recreation.

Pay attention to ambition and personal acquisition

But let's not lose sight of spiritual implications
Look unto God, who is our sustainer,
And be sincere, for we are his containers,
For if in this life only we have hope,
We would not be fit for heaven neither the earth.

Escape

Let me steal you out of there
To a place with margarita and gin
From that withering atmosphere
To where hearts flutter and heads spin

That smile will fade and suffocate
Unless my cavern's nostalgic aroma
Pushes you to dream and anticipate
The free open spaces of Oklahoma

Let me steal you out of there
And plant seeds in stylistic rhythm
Away from that dampen atmosphere
To live life to its fullest, on the brim

Beneath the bridge, down the slope
Hold my hand, run from that room
To the horizon, through the grove
From that godforsaken monsoon

Let me steal you out of there
From that incarcerated room of gloom
And go where the mountains peak, where
Air is cool and there are stars, and moon.

Me

If I should write about me
A flamboyant autobiography
Would I be an impressionist?
Could I be simply me?

Are colors always bright?
Does radiance refer to light?
Does dull paint pictures of gloom
Or is it in symphony with my tune?

If I should write about me,
I'd include my life's history.
Rough rivers, ominous clouds
Foaming seas; winding road,
Banquet halls, waterfalls,
Thorny rose on garden walls.

If I should write about me,
I'd include grace and mercy
For it was not my sobriety
That brought me prosperity

If I should write about me
I'd tell you things you didn't see
Like, my sarcastic tones
When I am home alone
And how stubborn I can be

If I should write about me
A flamboyant autobiography
Would I be an impressionist?
Could I be simply me?

The Three in Me

Who would you like to see?
The man I really am,
Or the man I pretend to be?
Who would you like to see?
The good? The evil? Or the naughty?

In the mirror I see a simple shell.
Deep in the eyes the soul will tell
Of pain and misery, extravagance and luxury,
Anger and cruelty, of peace and tranquility
Truth and reality, of love and loyalty
Of courage and mercy

But who would you like to see?
Will you edit if I expose the real me?
Will you dot my I's and cross my T's?
Can I let my hair down and really be me—
Open and publicly, unapologetically?

Me by myself, flexibility
With my family, peace and tranquility
Me at church, spirituality
At work, it's professionality

In my business, fervently
Different places different personality
When I try to do good, evil presents itself
When I do bad, I open the gates of hell
How complex how controlled
Who could tell if I withhold?

Now, can you handle this reality?
If you fire shots, I will dodge your bullets
If you play hardball, I will make you the menace

Yet with a thread, I'll be led over a precipice
What wretched man I am, the three in me
Not paranoid as you might think—
The world is ugly, and the matrix stinks.

Circle of Life
Morning by morning new mercies I see,
It's not by strength, it's not by might
It's not in the rigors or wars that men fight
Except God builds the house we waste our might
Except he watches the city the watchman to flight
And so, I muse on the thought...vanity of vanity
And sought for God in his power and his glory.

I saw the rich, living in elegance, pampered
And cared for with passion filled extravagance,
Lavishly adorned in costly apparel,
Dining sumptuously, creating his heaven in hell,
And I muse on the thought...vanity of vanity
And sought for God in his power and his glory.

I caught a vision of the poor, I observed the needy,
Hanging in the bulrush to maintain their sanity,
To keep things intact, their focus is on the needs
Of Maslow's Hierarchy, but God said, 'it's by faith,
Without which, it is impossible to please me.'
Though apparently miserable they fend to make
Ends bind, there's a peace that passes the understanding
Of the mind. And I muse on the thought, vanity
Of vanity and sought God in his power and his glory.

I focus on the wise; I took a look at the prudent,
For what was hidden from them was revealed
Unto little children. 'Doth not wisdom cry, and
Understanding put forth her voice?' I tried for an
Instant to find the relevance, and so, I look unto the
Wisest man to hear his opinion on what goes on beyond.
I settled for his conclusion on the whole duty of man,
And sought for God in the power of his resurrection
For vanity of vanity, all is vanity.

I took a look at the mentally deranged, and the
Academically deficient; I glance at the people
Without direction, and the spiritually impotent
I felt their hurt and absorbed their pain
And shiver at the thought that their parents to blame
Knowing it's a fact that this is inherent
For sin is the cause and death is the payment
And I muse on the thought...vanity of vanity
And sought for God in his power and his glory

There goes the proud and haughty
Here comes the fool, drunken in his folly
But I focus on the noble, being considered silly
Because he is filled with love and humility,
And I muse on the thought ...vanity of vanity
And sought for God in his power and his glory

I viewed the world; I appreciate humanity. I admire life
And embrace reality, but if it was not for God's grace
And his mercy, we all would be at one common place
And that's the cemetery for vanity of vanity, all is vanity.

I saw the bright lights; I viewed the kingdoms of men,
I considered the lilies, Solomon was not clothed like
One of them. And I knew from the beginning that all
Things must come to an end. So, seek God first, and
Eradicate the problem. When I looked at God's power,
And I saw his glory, I said to myself...morning by
Morning, I see new mercies.

from "Strong Men Cry, Too"

Life with my grandfather was unpredictable. When it was not one thing it was another. I will never forget the day that Gary, a boy at school, lied on me. We were in the fifth-grade at the time. Gary's parents had bought him a new leather belt. And he, wanting to show it off, took off his belt so everyone could see it. While we were walking to school, Gary called the children together to play a game we called Dutty Mumma (Dirty Mother). In this game, a girl would be selected—through a vote—to become the Dutty Mumma. The girl would pretend as though she was insulted by the name and would get a switch and use it to slap anyone in her path that called her Dutty Mumma; that is, if she could catch anyone in her path. This was a game we all loved and played for two reasons. The first reason we loved the game was that we, the boys, got to vote for the prettiest girl in the group—the one that we all liked—so that we would have the chance to tease her for being the Dutty Mumma. In my days, children did the craziest things when they liked each other. The second reason was that the chase by the Dutty Mumma guaranteed that we all got to school on time. Gary wanted to show off his new belt, so he initiated the game, changed the rules and gender roles of the game on the spot. And he, being a boy—and the loud spokesperson he was—selected himself without a vote and assumed the role of the Dutty Mumma. Then he took off his belt and began to chase the children on their way to school.

I was never a friend of Gary. I never liked the guy; therefore, I rebelled against the sudden changes. When I saw that I couldn't get enough votes to overrule Gary's autocratic ideas, I chose not to be a part of the game. The truth is, whether he had changed the rules or not, I would not have participated once he was in the game. I was not fond of Gary. He was the kid who Miss Lawrence, our fifth-grade teacher, relied on to tell her who was chatting in class behind her back while she wrote on the chalkboard. None of us boys—my friends in particular—in the classroom could stand Gary. We all disliked him. Gary always wanted to be the class prefect, but we never allowed him to get the role. My friends and I always voted against him and inspired others to follow suit when election time came around.

More importantly, Gary was the one who caused the summary of my fourth-grade report to say—too much talking. Of course I talked a lot in class, but the truth is, the teacher never caught me. Gary was the one who pointed me out every time she asked who was chatting. As a result, we always had private vendettas during the week in the classroom, and usually settled them with fistfights at the back of the schoolyard on Fridays after dismissal. This way, if a teacher saw us fighting on the weekend, by the time Monday came around, that teacher stood the chance of forgetting that we fought, and we would be free from punishments. Nevertheless, though none of us liked Gary, he never seemed to care. Therefore, we labeled him as an informer, and avoided him as best as we could.

On the day in question, we all got to school early. But it seemed as if Gary had not gotten enough attention for himself and his new belt; because, even during lunchtime, when the Dutty Mumma was not needed, Gary could be seen running around the playing field by himself like a dog chasing its tail. He horsed around wildly with his belt, lashing himself at times, saying giddy-up as if he was riding a horse. In the heat of his joviality and making a public spectacle of himself, Gary somehow lost the belt. I learned later, that he went home and told his parents that his belt was squeezing his waist and he took it off, placed it on the ground, and I stole it. That evening, his parents drove with him to our house, just as my tired grandfather came in from the farm. Because our house was always filled with guests, I paid little attention to the small group that came, until I heard my grandfather calling for me.

"Where is the belt you took from Gary at school today?" he

asked.

"Where is the what?" I asked, astonished, not understanding or believing what I was hearing. Then I realized that the visitors were Gary and his parents. I looked at him in shock, and he stared back at me, his eyes unblinking like the snake he was. Can you believe it? He stood right there in front of me, calm as a cobra, and lied through his teeth.

"Did you, or did you not, take Gary's belt when you were playing today?" asked my grandfather, stressing every syllable in every word and pausing at every comma as though he was punctuating the sentence while he spoke, and as though I had a problem understanding plain English.

"No Uncle Steve," I replied, "I was not even playing with Gary."

Uncle Steve turned away from me and promised Gary's parents that he would get to the bottom of what happened. But Gary's mother started a commotion. She lamented on how she had just bought the belt over the weekend when she visited Kingston, and how expensive it was, and that she could not sleep in peace if the belt was not returned. My grandfather asked her to bring him the receipt if she still had it in her possession and promised to reimburse her, but she kept on babbling. Her husband nudged her in the side as if he was trying to tell her that that was enough and that she was overdoing her little stint, but she was on a roll. She complained that the belt was not an ordinary one, that it was pure leather, the real cow skin, and that it was not sold in the countryside. She even told my grandfather how she wrapped the belt around her arthritis knee and left it there overnight and felt as fit as a fiddle the next day. She claimed the belt drew out the arthritis pain from her knee. When she realized that the healing virtue of the belt did not arrest my grandfather's attention nor affect his sympathy, she lectured him of the hassle it would take for her to travel to Kingston again to get the identical belt. The hassle, she claimed would have been unbearable and would cost her far more than the cost of the belt.

"But I never took his belt," I said, "I was not even in his game."

"Speak when you are spoken to," my grandfather warned, with renewed strength and vigor. My grandmother was silent the whole time. She appeared timid in front of Gary's strong and boisterous mother. She probably feared a confrontation or maybe she was ashamed, or in disbelief that her beloved grandson was becoming a thief. She looked at me doubtfully and searchingly as if to question if I really took the belt or not; then she drew me behind her to either shield or to usher me away from my grandfather's presence, I could not distinguish between the two.

"Come and apologize to these people!" my grandfather commanded, his voice in an angry roar.

"I don't know what to say," I said softly, but in strong opposition.

"You will say that you are sorry!" he yelled, his eyes glaring.

"But I did not take his belt, why should I be sorry?"

"Shut up and say that you are sorry! you lying rascal. Your own father will have to put you away in a juvenile detention camp."

"I am sorry," I said, in a croaky voice, picking my nails and hanging my head, knowing that to apologize was to acknowledge the wrong. Tears rolled down my face, not only in anticipation of the beating that I suspected would come, but the fact that Gary was victorious. A broad, sinister grin flashed across Gary's face as if he had received due diligence, but his mother was not satisfied with the results, so she kept on babbling. I walked away to my room halfheartedly when I was permitted to do so, and I wept bitterly.

My grandparents negotiated with Gary's parents and they settled in a way that I was not privileged to know. Then, after silently taking his shower, without the usual dramatic singing and whistle of contentment, my grandfather went to the local bar to have drinks with his friends, as was his custom. When he left the house, I was relieved. I thought the ordeal was over, and that the evil had passed, only to realize that he returned home prematurely and summoned me to his room.

He must have binged that night because the alcohol on his breath was enough to sedate a small child. Though I saw my grandfather as wicked, deep down I believed he was not capable of impulsive acts of violence; therefore, I believed he had to rely on a substance to numb his conscious senses, to give him courage, and to stimulate the aggression that was buried deep within his soul.

When I got to his room he grabbed me by the waistband, slammed me into the wall and used his body to slam the door shut behind me. His eyes were as red as blood and I must stress that the alcohol on his breath must have been above the legal limit because

I could hardly breathe. With his free hand, he pulled out the strip of car tire he had had under the edge of his mattress—the piece of car tire that he reserved for me—and beat me, mercilessly.

I screamed, tumbled, hollered, rolled, wiggled, and squirmed but he kept whacking me harder and harder. With the first few hits that he gave me, I screamed so hard at the top of my lungs, the peak of which I lost my voice, or probably my breath, but no sound came forth. Then, as the strip of car tire dug into my flesh, leaving cuts, bloodshot welts and bruises—like a siren—I found my voice again, and wailed. That evening my grandfather whipped me ten times as hard and as long as I have ever been whipped in my lifetime; it appeared to me as if I got lashes retroactively. It seemed, too, as though he was beating me for something that I had no knowledge of doing. In that, the longer the ordeal, the more epithets and expletives he uttered until he fell into a rhythmic pattern in which he grunted with the force of every blow. Then he slowed down as if he was out of breath—tired, I suppose—and we started a narrative in which he whacked me at the end of every clause.

"Did you take the belt?"—Whack!
"No Uncle Steve!"—Whack!
"You lying rascal."—Whack
"Help me, somebody. Help!"—Whack!
"What have you done with the belt?"—Whack!
"I don't"—Whack!
"Speak the truth, and speak it ever, cost it what it will."—Whack!
"Jesus Christ, Almighty God!"—Whack!
"Never you shout the Lord's name in vain,"—Whack! "Where is the belt?"—Whack!
"I don't know! I don't have it! I never took it!"—Whack! Whack! Whack!
"Tell the truth, you good for nothing wretch!"—Whack!
Even when I said nothing:
Whack!
Whack!
"I have it! I have it!"—
"Where is it?" he said, panting out of breath. His hand with the strip of car tire suspended in the air.
"It's at school!" I said, lying on myself for him to stop—Whack!

The Christian Soldier 171

Beaten to a pulp. Beaten mercilessly, I confessed to a crime I never committed. In that moment, my grandmother pushed on the door and with her bodyweight—a little too late—and braced the door open, sprang into the room, held onto my grandfather's hand, the whip which was coming down struck her; hence, she took the final hit for me.

"Enough! Steven, enough!" she screamed. "Are you going to kill him?" I had taken multiple hits to the head, my back, across my side, on my legs, and across my arms. My grandfather had beaten me like a slave, beaten me mercilessly with a piece of car tire, punished me severely for an act that I was not guilty of, an act for which I could not prove my innocence.

"We cannot spare the rod and spoil the child," he said, breathing heavily. "See, he confessed that he has the belt at school. I will have to go to the school with him for it tomorrow."

"Oh no you don't," replied my grandmother, "you do what you have to do, I will follow him to school," she said.

The next day my grandmother shamefully walked with me to school. Shamefully, because I am yet to find a parent who would walk proudly with a so-called thieving child. When we got to the school, I began to search the playing field with the hope that Gary had forgotten the belt there, but when I did not find it, I began to search into every nook and cranny I thought it possibly could have been. I walked and kicked up every cluster of leaves under the eucalyptus trees that lined the edge of the playing field, but the belt was not there. Then I went to search the undergrowth down the slope below the eucalyptus trees; my grandmother followed closely behind.

Nature was at its best that morning and I was at my worst. The morning sun had risen over the horizon and it glared on the school's playing field. The grass below the playing field was wet with dew. Small frogs jumped from the wet grass before I placed my feet on them. Lizards scampered up the branches of trees at my appearance. Butterflies hovered over wild rosebuds. Swarms of bees buzzed in the dugout hollow of a tree where they made their hive, and birds chirped melodiously as if they were singing morning hymns. Had it not been for my peculiar situation, I might have had a field day with the birds and my slingshot.

By this time, a small inquiring crowd had gathered on top of the hill overlooking the slope and Gary had joined in the midst. When he saw that it was my grandmother and I who were below them, he began to shout for other children to come and watch.

The crowd grew larger. My grandmother got frustrated. I was flustered. She picked a small branch from a nearby tree and smote me a few times and asked how come I could not find the belt. Each time she slapped me the crowd roared with laughter. Stricken with pain, I winced like a dying animal before its master. And though she was not hitting me as hard and as forceful as my grandfather had done, the swollen areas, cuts, and stale bruises I got the night before caused the pain from the branch to feel extremely excruciating.

I wobbled with every blow of the switch. The laughing children seemed to have had knowledge of why I was being beaten. Gary must have told them. But they did not care whether or not I was innocent or guilty. They were there for the fun of it. They all knew me, but that did not help. Nobody came to my rescue. A few of my close friends were there and they knew I would never have played with Gary much more to touch his property, but they watched in silence. And, as far as I knew it, none of them questioned Gary about the cause of his malicious actions. Nobody cared about Gary's motive. They never asked him why.

Gary was charismatic. He controlled the laughing crowd. He riled them up. They loved him. He led them like the leader of a mob in the stands of an arena. They shouted as if for blood revenge.

They were dramatic.

They were entertained.

Though I buckled under the pain, I was too ashamed to cry aloud in front of the laughing children. Tears streamed steadily down my face and though my heart was heavy, I resolved not to make any sound at all. She switched me a few times more and the crowd roared. I thought of Gary, clenched my teeth and ignored the pain that came from the branch she used. I swallowed hard and blinked my eyes, but I could not hold back the tears that rolled down and drenched my face.

I could have grabbed the switch from my grandmother because I believed I was stronger than her, but I did not. I could run away from her, like a gazelle, I could run, but I did not. I could have blocked the blows to lessen the effect, but I did not. Though she was hurting me, I stood steadily before her like a sheep before the shearer. I bowed down under the pain when I had to, but for the most part, I stood my ground in humility before her. I loved her still, even during the ordeal. She was still the only ally I had. I knew that she was standing in the gap for me when she volunteered to take me in search of the belt instead of allowing my evil grandfather to accompany me.

"I did not take his belt," I said softly, almost in a whisper, with an aching voice, gently pleading to my grandmother—my voice becoming hoarse—as I looked pitifully into her eyes. She dropped the branch frightfully as if she had absorbed the truth and the deep sadness that emitted from my spirit, and she looked at me as though she had wronged me and wanted to apologize. She raised me up, and then she straightened out my khaki shirt.

"Will you be okay?" she asked, further straightening out my shirt. I nodded in acknowledgement, but with a heavy heart; perfused tears gushing down the contours of my face. She ushered me to my classroom while telling me that she was going to come up and speak with my classroom teacher. As I walked up the slope and towards the class, the crowd that Gary had gathered became silent and slowly parted to let me through. I walked through their midst, head high, shoulders squared, and looked straight ahead, while tears gushed down my face.

I did not participate in class that day. I never even chatted with my friends. I simply sat down in the classroom and gently rubbed the swollen areas and the bruises on my arms and legs. I never even had lunch that day. Except for bathroom breaks, I never left the classroom. Every minute I thought about the incident a fresh stream of tears ran down my face.

At one point the teacher saw my teary face and must have heard the quiet sniffling, and instead of sympathizing with me, she smiled at me and asked me if I wanted to share something with the class—can you believe it? I knew that she must have heard the story from my grandmother, because my grandmother said that she was going to talk to her, so it must have meant that she was mocking me and was probably happy that it was one of the quietest classes that she had, since I was not talking with my friends. I shook my head and indicated that I did not want to share with the class. So, she walked by me and dropped a box of Kleenex tissues on my desk without saying a word and continued teaching.

In that moment, I wanted to grab Gary by the throat and strangle him on the spot. I thought of a hundred possible ways to punish him, but I could not find any that matched his crime. That day, all I thought about was revenge. I wanted a memorable revenge on Gary, but none of the methods I conjured up brought me the level of satisfaction I relished. As far as I can remember, I spoke once that day, to one boy and one boy only. I spoke to Gary. I vowed with an oath, and calmly told him that, as sure as night-followed day, if it was one day before I died, I was going to kill him. The teacher heard, moved Gary's seat to the front of the class, and brought me to the guidance counselor's office.

from "Stone Speech"

The lights from the brightly lit streets of Queens, New York, faded and blurred into a trail of taillights as his Lincoln Town Car barreled down the Belt Parkway onto the dark Southern State Parkway. He slowed to pass the police post at Exit 17 before he accelerated down the next two exits. Feeling lucky he escaped the sleeping police he smiled and floored the gas pedal. He switched from the far-left lane without signaling, cutting off every driver in his path and came off the highway at Exit 19 leaving behind a wail of car horns from disgruntled drivers. He then sped around the 15 miles per hour turn at thrice the speed, drove down Peninsular Blvd, and rolled up in the driveway of his rental apartment on Front Street, Hempstead.

He switched off the headlights, looked at his watch, cursed under his breath, then pushed his seat back and lowered the backrest. His heavy breathing was louder than the Redemption Song that came from the stereo. Sighing incessantly, he cut the engine and restlessly alighted from the car. It was now 4:00AM. He opened the house door and stepped in, dropped his keys beside a half-eaten slice of pizza on the kitchen table, glanced at the pile of dirty dishes in the sink, shook his head, and walked towards his bathroom. Moments later he was in the shower singing Redemption Song.

His apartment was a rat's nest—bed sheets in a crumbled pile on one side of his bed, and clothes scattered on the floor. Postcards, lotto tickets, and empty beer bottles on a center table. An ashtray filled with cigarette butts on his chest of drawers, and a steady line of black ants crawling from a crack beneath the window to the dead cockroach on his floor. He came out of the shower, scuffled through the drawers, pushing the rags aside. A ripped box of Durex fell to the floor, he grabbed and stuffed it beneath the clothes, select running gears, decked himself, before going out again.

Leaving the car behind, he jogged down Front Street to Uniondale, as silent as a cat's paw, and trotted off energetically towards her house. When he got there, he searched the flowerpot and under the doormat; not finding the keys he sought, he ran his fingers on top of the door-jam and got lucky. He pushed the keys into the lock and opened the door delicately and entered her house. The concrete wall evidenced his presence. The rattling key in the door lock captured her attention, she swirled around from the stove, froze at the sound, and looked intensely at the door—the spatula fell from her hand as the door cracked open.

And, as though she was uncertain what to do, she slowly wiped her hands in her apron and walked frightfully from the kitchen as he entered. Then she froze at the sight of him. He stared at her, longingly. She looked at him with fire in her eyes, unadulterated, impassioned, and aggressive. The early morning air seeped in. Bacon popped in the frying pan. The kettle whistled softly. He held her gaze and slowly but methodically unzipped and took off his sweatshirt. The muscles in his chest twitched as he bared them. She took a step backward clutching and pulling her blouse over her brassiere-less breast. He threw the shirt from him. It fell on a nearby chair. She rushed towards the bedroom, and he hurled forward and crashed into her, bouncing the dressing table to the side. The decorative vase on the dressing table tumbled to the hardwood floor—it broke and sent red petals and white glass into several directions.

He kicked the dressing table to one corner and pinned her against the wardrobe—one hand at her neck and the other at her groin. Muttering and gasping, face crushed against each other's, she wrestled frantically to free herself from his grasp. And, as though she mustered new strength, she grabbed him by the belt, whisked him around, and slammed his back against the shaking wardrobe. The picture of Jesus and the twelve disciples rattled, loosened, spiraled downward and crashed into the mixture of red and white.

I glanced at the fallen picture—shattered streaks and cracks ran down the middle separating the disciples, but the glass was held together by the frame. I looked back at the two. He was tall, clear-skinned, and ugly. He had a killer instinct—aggressive and desperate. The hungry look in his eyes revealed his intention. He grimaced and held her tighter. Sweat glistened on his elongated face. They fell on the couch; fighting breathlessly.

The leathered couch crackled and screeched.

The kettle whistled violently, the phone rang, the scent of charred bacon drifted in the dimly lit room.

A raggedy mutt yelped and scratched at the room door, but they ignored the tumult. He fought her with fervor and intensity until he ripped the clothes from her body; grunting each time he jolted her. And, as if to reciprocate his actions, her head flew back and forth rhythmically with each jolt. Hands still at her throat, her soft screams muffled into moans.

In the midst of the tumult, I watched. He was on top of her stretched out body, he jolted her again and again, and in a wave-like motion her body reciprocated his actions. She closed her eyes and purred listlessly as though the breath had left her body, then she melted under his power. She was as a lamb to the slaughter. Silenced. He manhandled her like a skilled craftsman—shifting and positioning her at intervals. He bared his teeth cannibalistically and gnashed at her neck, betwixt her breast, down her navel and up again.

He looked down at her limp body and smiled victoriously as though he savored the delight. Then, he angled her. Heaved his head, pumped his groin, and grunted. Heaving, grunting, and pumping. Heaving, grunting, and pumping—like a piston, he was pumping. She came alive again and her soft purrs became pants, reciprocated grunting, groaning, and back to moaning. It was as though she was in a delightful dilemma and blissful pain.

And, like a pensive bystander, unaroused, I watched.

He jolted her a few more times; faster and faster yet. And, with each jolt, the couch bounced against the wall with a squeak and a thud. The dog yelped louder and louder. The squeaking, crackling, yelping and the momentary thud must have irritated him, he glanced up and stared in my direction threateningly as though he had discovered my presence and as though I was responsible. Then he creased his lips, trenched his eyebrows and shouted, "Shut up Rex!" The dog whined and went silent.

She joined him and looked in my direction. Then, with one hand on his gluteus maximus and the other at the back his neck, she pulled him onto her again and he continued their act.

I wondered. Did he just call me Rex? Or, did he refer to the mutt? The audacity of him! Did she tell him of our relationship? How she banged me at nights, that she confessed all her faults in my hearing? Did she tell him that I am always there in the wee hours when he was not? That my ears never failed, and I never interrupted her while she spoke? Did she share our secrets?

He swallowed hard and turned to look at me again; this time, questioningly. If it were possible, cold sweat might have washed me, or I probably would have messed my pants and whimper at such a stare. The guy was like a beast. It seems as though he thought I made the interventions. As though I had magical powers to make the phone ring, the picture fall, or the bacon burn.

At the top of the hour, they suddenly began to whisper, and to laugh. And, in-between whispers and laughs, he gently kissed her on the forehead. And, after what seemed like an eternity of cuddling, she got up, walked over to his shirt, held it up like a flying flag—twiddling it on her fingers, then she tossed it to the victor. Apparently, she had surrendered. He was her colonizer; she was his slave, held together by dark emotions. He must have placed his mark deep into her fleshy soul, a mark that suggested he owned her.

She slipped from the room and back again with a drink in her hand, it was as though that was his reward. He shared his prize with her.

Made in the USA
Coppell, TX
08 February 2026